D1169269

IN SEARCH OF MIDNIGHT

THE MIKE MCGEE HANDBOOK OF AWESOME

BY MIKE MCGEE

A Write Bloody Book
Nashville. Los Angeles. USA

WRITE BLOODY PUBLISHING
NASHVILLE, TN

In Search of Midnight: The Mike McGee Handbook of Awesome
by Mike McGee

Write Bloody Publishing ©2009
1ˢᵗ printing.
Printed in NASHVILLE, TN USA

In Search of Midnight: The Mike McGee Handbook of Awesome Copyright 2009.
All Rights Reserved.

Published by Write Bloody Publishing.

Printed in Tennessee, USA.

No part of this book may be used or performed without written consent from the
author, if living, except for critical articles or reviews.

Cover Designed by Joshua Grieve: paperplanemedia.com
Interior Layout by Lea C. Deschenes
Type set in Helvetica Neue and Bell MT
Edited by Derrick Brown, shea M gauer, Saadia Byram, Michael Sarnowski
Proofread by Jennifer Roach

To contact the author, send an email to writebloody@gmail.com

MORE PRAISE FOR MIKE MCGEE

Man, you are hilarious!
　　　—Sinbad, Comedian

Mike McGee is love.
　　　—The Denver Spoken Word Scene

*Mike McGee is the funniest man I know. For two years straight
I have begun laughing in the middle of a meditation course at
the mere thought of him, approaching me with that knowing
warmth and love inside his bubbling, joyful reminders of how
incredible it is to be alive.*
　　　—Buddy Wakefield, Poet

*Mike McGee is a ventrical revolutionary. His poems speak
directly to our blood. Intimate, funny and deeply touching, this
book reflects his generous and loving spirit. He is a poet that
everyone should have on their shelf and in their lives.*
　　　—Amber Tamblyn, Author/Actor/Activist

Short of hitting him over the head with a mallet, stealing his wallet and then eating a small piece of him, Mike McGee's latest book provides all the information one needs to become almost as awesome as Mighty Mike McGee himself. This tasty tome is as good as nachos, nature's perfect food.
  —Shappy Seasholtz, Poet/Comedian/Asshole

Years from now, historians and underfed grad students alike will wonder what it was like to be a poet on the road in the early aughts. All they need to do is read this book and remember to keep their voices down: librarians don't like sustained hysterical laughter, even if there is a darn good reason for it."
  —Cristin O'Keefe Aptowicz, Author of *Words In Your Face: A Guided Tour throughout Twenty Years of the New York City Poetry Slam*

5

DEDICATION

This collection of my work is dedicated to my mother, Becky McGee, and the siblings she gave me: Jamie, Christina, Catalina, Olivia, and Shannon. They taught me love and laughter. They are my sweetest nuggets.

This book is also dedicated to the women who, before leaving this world, planted and watered my love of life, people, humor, and words: Great-grandma Alice, Grandma Mary, and my aunts Dawn and Molly.

FOREWARD

Mike is very much a live poet. What you are about to read should be read to you, or by you to someone else. Mike is a damn good writer, but he is one of the world's best talkers. And this talk is not all fart noises and whale impressions. While he is very funny, he is not just funny. His work is an examination of both the banality and the glory that we do all the hours we aren't sleeping. It speaks to his constant search for meaning when most would have gone to rest in comfort or cynicism.

As one of his many buttons state: I like Mike. More than that, I like that Mike exists.

His spirit is indivisible from his style; his will is completely intertwined with his work. He is hilarious without effort and sincere without pretense. What he writes is more a love letter to the world than to himself.

The Mighty Mike McGee makes me believe in people who, just by falling to earth, help fix it. While he could not out run a three-legged dog on heroin, much less a locomotive, he can write with a voice of such compassion and comic brilliance that the world becomes a much better place for having him in it.

Enjoy this book, because if you can't, there may be something seriously wrong with you.

—Geoffrey Jason Kagan Trenchard

IN SEARCH OF MIDNIGHT: THE MIKE MCGEE HANDBOOK OF AWESOME

"I will walk into the sunshine with you
or you will not be my friend.
I will instruct you and you will instruct me.
I will learn things from you and you will learn things from me.
Otherwise you can't be my friend."

– Robert Guillaume

RANDOM FACTS ABOUT MIKE MCGEE, PART I

In no specific order. Hence, random.

- ✸ I studied to be a Catholic priest until I was fourteen or fifteen. I was all set for seminary school, then I woke up and despised the church. I still look up to Father Shishida, who died some time ago, and Father Stout. They were good, honorable men.

- ✸ I like road trips with friends. Nothing like seeing the world together.

- ✸ I adore cornbread, but I despised it as a child. I am still repulsed by creamed corn.

- ✸ On January 8, 1998, I creeped out Jon Stewart in the hallway of The Improvisation on Melrose in West Hollywood. I was dressed like a douche bag tourist (Hawaiian shirt, khaki shorts, white socks and velcro sandals) and asked him for his autograph even though he could tell I couldn't remember his name. I was taller than him and twice his weight, moving ever within a foot of space to him. I was a douche bag tourist. I also met Drew Carey that night and he was the nicest guy ever. Ever. Tied with "Weird" Al Yankovic for being the nicest entertainers I've met.

- My estranged maternal grandfather was buddy-buddy with George Herbert Walker Bush in the 1980s. I met my grandfather once.

- Until I discovered spoken word and comedy, I really wanted to be a hip-hop emcee.

- Seaweed wrap (nori) is one of my favorite snacks. Big time.

- As a child, I won a dozen or so talent shows by lip-syncing with puppets. I studied ventriloquism as well. I am bringing back the lip-syncing and puppets.

- While I may look Scottish and Irish, and my last name has roots in both cultures, I am only aware of about 70% of my heritage, which is über-mutt. Too many orphans in my lineage to ever really know the rest.

- I thoroughly enjoy Garth Brooks. 'Nuff said.

- I can count to six in Vietnamese.

THE END

If I should die today
I hope I've done all the laughing
I can let out of this body
I hope it was heard, appreciated and contagious

I hope a great many people remember
the fact that I was here

Not remembered like
Shakespeare or Mussolini
Remembered more along the lines of
a much simpler person
like Gandhi . . . Albert Gandhi
who lived down the street from me and
loved food and women as if
they were oxygen and humor. . . .

Humor
as in
there is no Albert Gandhi that I know of
I made him up and
that's funny to me

If I die today
I want the world to be able
to go on without me

Even though I know
it will be incredibly hard

If I die today
I should be cremated
or properly stuffed
because I would make one fabulous
lawn gnome scarecrow

It really doesn't matter what is done with my remains
but please
do not auction off my genitalia
or I will haunt you with dick jokes
for the rest of your life

If I should die today
I hope those who knew me well
will tell the world that I was
rarely ever serious
  that inciting laughter was always
  my primary goal
    that by experiencing
    someone else's joy

    I lived it as well

When ordering my tombstone
please have the date of my death
span three or four days
  I want people to think of it

as a big event they may have missed out on

McGee-A-Palooza

If I die today
I want everyone
I've loved and liked
to know that I've
appreciated them very much
    you've made this world
    a hell of a lot more tolerable
        I hope my life was worth your time
        as yours was worth every second of mine

Should I die today
make note that I
am not ready for it
but I've accomplished
centuries in my decades and
for that I am grateful

So please enjoy tomorrow for me

If you can hear this
You're invited to my funeral
especially if you promise to
shut the fuck up every
once in a while and just listen
    to keep fighting the good fight
    to always do what is right

and before you go
tell the sun I said hello and
        kiss the moon goodnight

PROGRESS FACILITY (SANTA CLARA, CALIFORNIA 2008)
Seek out real change. It keeps us going.

I MAILED MYSELF A LOVE LETTER YESTERDAY

I mailed myself a love letter yesterday
I can't wait to get it back
to see what's going in my life
    to see how my relationship with myself
    is developing
Yesterday I learned of all my
faults and casualties
Tomorrow I will come to grips with how great I am
Next week I will begin teaching
courses in coolness where water
can enroll itself to learn
how to become ice cubes

When I'm thirty-five
I may run for President
bringing back facial hair as the symbol of a good leader
I could be the first President of the United States
to get elected without a campaign budget
but instead
with the help of small woodland animals
    who control the winds of change

I will have
    Gomez
    Neil Diamond
    Neil Young

The Roots
RC Weslowski
Myself
and Sigur Ros
perform at my inauguration

The White House will serve ramen noodles 24 hours a day

On tap

I believe I am living my life to the fullest
but I have to accept the fact that
there are others whose lives
are much fuller than mine
I will make up for it
with my lack of hunger
I will catch up

If I change my name to Robin Hood
I can steal from the rich and give to the poets
I can wear tights and people will
finally understand me
because deep down I'm a chubby ballerina
with a penchant for dictionaries
late-night television and
fuzzy slippers

Weirdos
should look weird
This will be my uniform

Yesterday I felt like a singer
with a song I couldn't sing

Today I'm a father who
can never have children

Tomorrow rests inside a full night's sleep
for billions of lovers and fighters
who love to fight about
everyone else on the planet

Sometime ago I promised myself that
I would always put things down on paper
    whether they were letters to women
    who never knew I loved them
    or in sticky notes to bullies
    demanding their immediate surrender

*"Give us one week, my little nerdlings, and the talkers will take
    down the entire school"*

It's not easy to convince a table of nerds
to fight without a twenty-sided die
but I'm confident that a good bark can stop any bite

I promised myself many, many years ago
    that I would never settle for average or mediocre
    that I would always try to find the best and worst
    within myself and maybe I'd be able

to work the two out so they could learn from each
other

It's one thing to say that I'm worthy of love
It's another thing to say that I'm worthy of my own

Here I am, alone
with all this love to give and
it seems as though I'm still trying
to find myself so I know who to give it to

I've lived a life with
such varied confidence
so I mailed myself a love letter yesterday
    It was just a dress rehearsal
    so that I would know how to
    respond to the women who've told me that
        I'm ugly
        or I'm a great friend
        or I'm just like one of the girls (shit)

I know I'm not tall, dark & handsome
but two* out of three ain't bad

    *now you're probably wondering which two I'm
    talking about
    (but I only need one woman to figure that out on her
    own)

Most women say all they really want is
a man with a good sense of humor

LIARS

I'm a 5' 6" stack of bad-ass
which is just the right height
for a man who loves life
so if I'm gonna find a girl that
    digs me with life's biggest shovel
then I'm just gonna have to learn to dig myself first

THE WAFFLE TRUTH

If God presented
itself to you
in the form
of a waffle
and said

*"Marty, I've got a plan for you!
Tell the world of my imminent return!"*

Would you answer to the name Marty and
do as God commanded?

Or

Would you cover God in syrup and
finish your breakfast?

MANHATTAN MANGO BEAR (FOR KAREN), (NEW YORK, 2004)
Tastes good on waffles and New York!

METHODS FOR BEING NICE

Being a shitbox to others is easy and probably instinctual. For nice people, the practices listed below are almost second nature. That's not to say they aren't worked on and failed at by nice folks everyday. Nice people also have to work at being nice.

⊛ Be attentive. Recognize the importance of what people tell you. Memorize faces, names, and dates. You'll probably surprise them with your recalling and informative abilities. Everyone wants to be remembered. Be one of the ones who does the remembering. Your efforts will not go unnoticed.

⊛ Be generous. Splurge. Cover a meal from time to time. Help someone move. Get up and give. If you can afford it and someone very much needs it, then help out. Always need over want. Always. Always. Always.

⊛ Be calm. Never show anger unless absolutely necessary. It can and will be necessary in life, but most of our displays of anger are reactionary, showy and uncalled for, nor do they benefit anyone within earshot.

⊛ Be real. If you keep up with your niceness activities

and practices, people will spread the word, but only if they feel it's genuine. If being nice doesn't feel right to you, then it won't be and people will notice.

⊛ Be honest. The absolute best policy. Never take undeserving credit for anything. Never allow false representation of your views and policies. Never deny someone a deserved compliment. Always be willing to say the truth to everyone who needs it. Always admit when you are wrong, but never when you aren't.

⊛ Be thorough. Practice niceness every day. Allow yourself time alone. Be social, helpful and courteous, but know when you're not needed.

⊛ Be available. Be approachable. Let people talk and be sure to listen as much as possible. Give them a channel to contact you through if they need an ear down the road.

Other Duhs:
⊛ Learn to cook and do it often for others. Feed the hungry!
⊛ Make sure people get home safely.
⊛ Be an authority, but always defer to an expert.
⊛ Open doors for people. Offer your seat to anyone.
⊛ Be kind to all strangers.

A WORD FROM MIKE MCGEE

Came up with this word around Thanksgiving 2004.

adual (a-d'u-al) *adj.*
Of or relating to the individual characteristic of being, having originated as a natural pair, wherein the subject is isolated due to the separation from, or destruction of, its original mate.

"The farmer stared at his adual hand, gripping the tractor's steering wheel at the 10 o'clock position."

adually (a-d'u·al·ly) *adv.*

aduality (a-d'u-al-i'ty) *n.*
The quality or character of being a singular part of a natural pair, former or anti-dichotomy.

"She had lived in aduality since her twin sister died."

SWEET RIDE (COLUMBUS, OHIO 2006)
This car is orange. I love orange. Feel free to fill it in with your favorite color. Share that color with others.

DOWN ON THE CORNER (VANCOUVER, BRITISH COLUMBIA 2008)
Sometimes it's good to just stand on the corner and watch things go by. It's also good to visit this neighborhood in East Vancouver. I highly recommend checking it out. Tell them McGee sent you.

WHEN LADYBUGS ARE TEMPTED

It is not always my job
to be bigger than people.

Today I am a six-legged insect
with wings of clipped red nails.

Sometimes Mama Nature asks
creatures like me to
ladybug our way toward surprised
9-to-5 *cubicly happy* people and wait.

They'll be eating lunch on outdoor patios,
sharing stories about a job
they are slowly escaping from
and what things they're gonna do this summer
with people they'd rather not do things with.

When the time is all wrong, and
They've forgotten my presence
    somewhere between their second unspoken cocktail and
    first real lunch-break confessional,
I tell them that:
- 🏵 four college students died for their sins in Ohio back in
  1970
- 🏵 war is the biggest way to say you're right, but it can
  never be unanimous proof

✵ children and small animals know who you really are at
  home

I'll be much too small to say it aloud
so I'll spell it out to them in spilled salt and
when Nancy, the over-worked
Human Resources Manager
sees my message,
she'll brush it off the table
before any of her coworkers see it,
keeping it to herself forever
after shooing me away from
the remains of her meatless Caesar salad.

She'll go back to work
and she won't get much done
other than thoughts of vacations that pay,
exploring the horizon while barefoot
and finally trying that spicy Middle Eastern food
she's suddenly not so scared of.

Sometime toward the end of my short, full life
I might forgive her for being so selfish with my earlier
    messages.

I will have six-legged sons;
Nancy will have upright girls.
Both families will visit
more open spaces than buildings
and they will do it together

naturally, but unwittingly.

The humans will still eat foods
too easy to be real and
too fast to be good for them

She will allow her children
to say bad things to strangers because
she will still assume
that all children are innocent and
couldn't possibly mean what they say

One day, while picnicking
at a park with a larger segment of her family,
in a state of truly sudden, irrational human fear
one of Nancy's infant daughters
will react violently to
my favorite son landing on her toy.

As my son attempts to communicate with her,
she will scream and slap at him awkwardly,
abstracting my son's bloody remains
onto her hand and forearm,
and as Nancy blindly rushes to her child's aid,
never knowing the crime
her offspring committed to mine,
my family will fly in at speeds and
strengths we never let humans observe
then swiftly lift the giggling child up and away
bringing her to me.

I will paint her nails red with
my son's blood and wings,
whispering to her all the names of
future men who will simply be there for her
    in ways not unlike taller
    upright versions of my son,
        not as red as he
        but willing to give blood.

For our short time with her,
we will call her by a new name
and it will sound like (insert insect phrase),
which translates to
    new double-footed tiny giant,
then we will teach her to truly crawl.

Maybe many years later
while cleaning us off with
a gas station squeegee,
she will remember our time together and
say a public prayer
remembering to crawl before ever lying down and
why she's always added a few black spots
to her daughter's red nail polish.

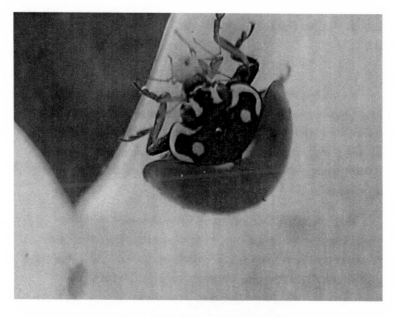

**LADYBUG OUTSIDE OF MY MOTHER'S HOUSE
(SILICON VALLEY, CALIFORNIA, 2008)**
This ladybug was tempted to punch me in the neck
until I presented it with a tiny shepherd's pie!

CONTRACTUAL OBLIGATION

With regard to a relationship that has met its end, it is an amazing act of selfishness to remove all traces of love from the outer world. It is also highly irresponsible for either party to pursue any act of retribution or revenge in conjunction with the intangible portions of the broken agreement.

To pretend a former loved one does not exist is regrettable and evil, especially when it is impossible to remove the love from one's heart, or to box those feelings and memories into one valve or artery. To limit the pleasure derived from the positive memories by replaying the negative aspects of the relationship is unproductive and detrimental to the heart and mind, and it may preclude any future dealings with the former partner.

It is illogical to allow these memories of love to incite anger or frustration. They are merely memories and are not actually current. It is mutually beneficial for the two parties involved to attempt some self-reconciliation of the negative reminiscences of the former relationship.

I agree that the memory of this love should shadow any residual contempt and feelings of loss garnered by the destruction of the bond agreed upon between myself and they with whom the former bond was created.

_____

Sign Here
(1st Party)

_____

Sign Here
(2nd Party)

_____

Sign Here
(Witness)

GEEZ, US!

I was hanging out with Jesus the other day
drinking grape soda on His balcony
We watched the sun go down beyond Los Angeles
I had hoped for wine
He said I should have brought some

We talked a lot
I asked Him what it was like to die
He said it was His favorite of all His Dad's art projects

> *Death is so quick compared to life*
> *because it is that awesome*

I asked Jesus what He liked about today and
it took Him too long to respond
I dozed off and dreamt of four men on Shetland ponies
riding around, breaking windows
  They were the Four Midgets of the Apocalypse
  They burned down miniature golf courses
  and stabbed people below the waist

Jesus woke me up and
presented me with an omelet
which was delicious
as any evening breakfast would be
when made by the Son of God

I told Him that He seemed like the cool older brother I
    never had
He thought that was cool and asked me to stop
    masturbating so much

I told Him that every day I feel a certain sense of
    unexplainable loneliness
He said it was because I spend too much time alone
I pondered that for a moment while He offered me hash
    browns

His apartment was decorated with film posters from movies
that told His story in some way
Last Temptation Of Christ
Jesus Christ Superstar
and Repo Man

One of the posters was signed by Willem Dafoe
He spoke well of Willem Dafoe
but Jesus doesn't own a DVD player

Over time
I got the feeling that the human part of Him wants to be forgotten
but the Heavenly side is anxious to introduce everyone to
    His Dad

I asked Him why He moved to L.A.
He said it was the hidden beauty
    That having to search for the good
    meant that when it was found
    it had to be authentic
He also pointed out that L.A. is one of the few places

a man dressed like Him can still go unnoticed in public

We watched Mexican television
He interpreted all of the game shows and soap operas
It stayed warm well into the night
so I slept on the balcony
while Jesus wandered the streets
looking for lost souls

In the morning
He woke me to another omelet
this time wrapped in a big flour tortilla
I wasn't hungry so He wrapped it and put it in a bag

Then He asked me to shave His head
I felt uncomfortable
He said it was okay
and that His strength came from somewhere else
He just wanted to fit in with the rest of us

I shaved His head
and waddled home

Later that afternoon
I noticed one of His hairs stuck to my collar
If I had a girlfriend and she found it before me
she might wonder who it came from
    but I don't
    and she can't
    and so she won't

I pulled out the breakfast burrito

and birthed it from its aluminum foil
I noticed a face burned into the tortilla
A surprising miracle for me to enjoy
He knew I wouldn't share it with anyone else

It made me wonder how often Jesus
promoted Himself with food items
For every one hundred new Starbucks
that opens around the world
a statue of Him cries chocolate milk

I ate my holy burrito neck first
and smiled
once I realized
that it was actually the face of Willem Dafoe

CHRISTMAS ALONG THE PACIFIC COAST HIGHWAY (CALIFORNIA 2006)
It doesn't matter who made the beauty, just be glad you get to see it.

SLEEPWALKER
(FOR MAUREEN)

I've been told it can be dangerous to wake up someone while they're sleepwalking. I believe it is far more disturbing to be awake, alone and motionless. Sleep has always felt like an incredible waste of time to me. Distance has always been a challenge to be covered, and if forever is a far-off town, and you live in said town, and you want me to live in said town with you, and if a town can be founded on a population of two, and the city center is really just our bed, then we can sleepwalk without moving and say without speaking all that should be said, and if what needs to be said is worth saying, then I'm laying it on the line as we speak. I must keep moving toward you, especially when I'm weak. So I will walk and eat. Walk and sing. Walk and chew gum at the same time. I will walk and sleep with my eyes open to the hope and dream that this distance between us, akin to the distance between thunder and lightning, will some day be a little less frightening—once I can see you. Once I can take you by the hands and say that no matter how you lay your arms, they make a doorway to the only home that can heal the holes in this heart and head. Lady, I've been waiting for you for so long, I've learned to sleep standing in this lifeline, and I'm fine, but I can't stand sleeping knowing you stay up at night, afraid to dream the dreams of me in the starring role of the sleeper hit of the slumber. So this summer will pass and at long last, I will return to you, to lay your head across my chest. Just know that the best dreams I've ever had are the ones I have in store for us when we're both awake.

ARTIST BOY

Hey, baby.
Do you like to cuddle?
Yeah, you know, make with the spooning.

Cause I'm an artist and
I want to share my futon with you.

Let's wear meaningless logos and
statements on t-shirts
thrift store pants and
get no more than
three body parts pierced or tattooed.
    You should get that tribal band
    around your arm covered up first.
    It is awfully trendy

I'll hinder my eyesight with my
unwashed, wavy, medium-length hair
while you smoke clove cigarettes and
we can admonish
everything bad in the world
all from the safety of our
independent coffee shop.

We'll complain about the country and
use red flag words like foreign policy

and do nothing about it other than
threaten to move to Canada or Amsterdam.

Commitments are for losers.
You and I should just be
who we are in public
then worry about us
when we're
alone.

We work together
cause you're an Aquarius
and I'm a Gemini
and they so totally
complement each other
    and who cares if they don't!
    Maybe we're the two that can make it work.
We can demolish all preconceived notions
with regard to astrology!

Plus! The novel I'm working on and
    your electric cello
are going to change the world

You and I are so *humble*
the world *needs* us.

Come with me to my loft at
my uncle's house;
we can smoke from my

hookah and watch my
David Lynch collection.
I'll ignore you for a while
until you throw yourself at me.
    Then we'll see where
    things go from there

We love the nothing.
And for this
the world needs more artists.
I am artist boy.
Get with me. Or don't.
I don't care.
I'm just an observer

    in
    this

lonely
    lonely
        world.

The Darkness imprisons us all
but the trees of truth
will tear it all down.

FIN.

SELF-PORTRAIT (SAN JOSÉ, CALIFORNIA 2005)
Taking a break from supreme creativity
to showcase the beauty of the artist himself.

PUDDIN'

This is a love poem, but not to any person, people, place, or position.

No. This is a love poem to a specific substance—one we're all familiar with, but rarely consider during moments of *nasty*. That substance is *pudding*.

Ladies and gentlemen, I need you to pretend you're not here for these words, for they are very personal. I am concerned with your safety. Those experiencing pangs of hunger, I urge you to get a snack immediately, for this is about to become *porn for fat people*.

Those of you who willing to experience gourmet eroticism, please, visualize along with me.

Picture a buffet unlike any other, where beautiful people of your dreams have gathered to feed you the silky delicacy known as pudding. Imagine that they are all so enveloped by ecstasy, so into the feast, they keep referring to this magnificent substance as "puddin." So drawn to it, they forget the letter G.

I would like to take a moment to speak to directly to that for which this poem was written:

Hello, pudding.
>   Oh, how I miss you, baby.

How I long to be near your bowl
>   with a very tiny spoon
>   so that I can take my time and enjoy you.

To caress your shapeless existence.

To watch you do that gelatinous jiggle you do
>   just before I consume you with all the passion
>   I learned from Bill Cosby himself.

Goddamn you, pudding!

How dare you disguise yourself!
Who will you be tonight, my sweet?
>   Maybe a bowl of Tapioca?
>   A taste of butterscotch?
>   Or will you be more complex?
>>   Donning a vanilla-chocolate ripple
>>   hiding away in my freezer
>>   hugging a stick
>>   and only succumbing to the name Pudding Pop!

Ohhh, pudding!

Temptation is for the weak. So please, call me Weakly
Weakerson when I am near you. Me and my band, The
Weaktones, will play you songs of desire and merriment.

If that doesn't work for you, my dear, sweet pudding, I can always put on my Marlon Brando costume.

BRANDO: *The one that seems to turn you on the most. The one that gets you all thick and creamy.*

Oh, pudding! I could just drink you from a huge vacuum hose
       out in my front yard
               naked (of course!)
                      in an inflatable kiddie pool
                            full of you.

The envy and confusion of those walking by would make it worth the effort. It is inherent to be jealous of someone else's bulk-ass pudding.

[We interrupt this poem to bring you viable content in an attempt to make this poem more accessible to a broader audience.]

Peace in the Middle East. Holla at a playa. Word to the nerd. My father never loved me.

I wanna make a difference. I suck. You suck. The government sucks.

[Now back to the poem already in progress.]

I could cover myself with you, and go as you to a

masquerade ball. People will want to lick you off of me—they always do—but I will say, *"No, I will lick me! For I have a tongue—my own tongue—and a book on yoga!"*

However, our love is limited, Pudding, for I have discovered that my body cannot tolerate our passion much longer. For you are composed with a blood of milk and sugar, and I should rather die than make you with water and sweetener.

So let us call for one last night of *nasty*—a grand finale—for I will now goodbye by summoning the spirit of Bill Cosby to say to you this:

COSBY: *Zibba zang, tazza beeza damn! Hah! Because, Wednesday is hump day. Kodak moment, hah!*

In conclusion, my dearest, sweet pudding, just know that forever I will spell love:

P-U-D-D-I-N…I forget the next letter . . . but know that my love for you
will never be consumed.

GRAVEYARD SHIFT

I've heard stories that
in 1500s England
they buried people prematurely
due to a comatose state caused
by drinking alcohol
from lead and pewter cups

To eradicate these awful mistakes
and to prevent many wrongful deaths
they hired men to sit in
cemeteries with lanterns and shovels
to listen for ringing bells
These bells were tied to twine
    the twine ran underground to
    the wrist of the deceased
If the person awoke
    inside their coffin
    and scrambled for escape
their bell would sound
six feet above and
the diggers would start digging
Hence, those buried alive were
saved by the bell
and the diggers worked what became
known as the first graveyard shift
The only people at that time

willing to work in the dark and
sleep during the day

So I'm at my new
graveyard job at the mall
I stock toys for the kiddies
I work in the dark like Quasimodo
because they would never
hire me for a daylight position
I guess I just don't appeal
to their regular shoppers
and I definitely don't appeal
to the kind of people
that stop by our store after
spending a few grand at Nordstrom

Come see the big hairy guy
Come one, come all
Come down to the mall
See for yourself
The big giant elf

I could never dance for a
dollar and I won't give up my
dreams for a job
I work in the dark to enjoy the sun
I plan my life during
my ten-minute breaks
while the nocturnal animals play
in the empty parking garage

amongst the littered
shopping bags, receipts and price tags

As the world sleeps
dreaming of designer clothes
bottled water and
beverly hills lifestyles
I debate with myself whether
I have time
    to
    suck down
    one more cigarette

If you can see
the blue of my collar
then you must know that
I have learned quite well
just how to differentiate between
    the day walkers and
        those that roam the night

I prefer the light of the moon over
your basic fluorescent office fixture
The kind of light that assumes a
distrust between you and your boss
    The kind of light
    that peeks into and
    around every corner
Those are the lights the stores at malls use
To scare away the shoplifters and

those are the lights they
shut off when the graveyard shift
punches in
They know that something will be
missing in the morning, so
what's the fucking point

The graveyard shift is creative
    Taking what is never rightfully
    theirs, but obviously no one else's either

There is always something so
missing when the
morning crew takes over
that the customers can
smell it under the hot
lights of omniscience

It is the creativity born with nightwalkers
It is how much the day hates the night

You'll never see a pigeon
hanging out with an owl

You'll never see Beverly Hills
hand me her phone number
as she leaves the mall with
her bags of
    "Hey, look at me!"

while I enter the mall in an air of

Hey…
look at me…

We're all the same, Beverly
Only you look really hot in that
outfit, the way it exposes your
midriff and your flat, flat stomach

I just wish you could say to me

You look good in that dictionary
the way it exposes your
ideals and manipulations
your faults and your ambitions.

We seem to take two different
escalators to get to the
same place in life
I'm kind of like banished royalty
and you're upper class white trash

Day and night can
never make love
They can only
tease each other
in a foreplay
they call twilight

The only things I regret
at three in the morning
as I solve the world's problems and
chain smoke outside the mall
are that I have no bell to ring
and rainbows never
come out at night

AIRPORT ESCALATOR (SOMEWHERE ELSE 2007)
Going downtrodden.

WORDS THAT SHOULD BE ACCEPTABLE IN SCRABBLE™

⊛ **fidoscillate**; (fyd' oss ill 8) *v.* – act of cooling off hot foods and drinks by setting them on one's head while spinning hand in hand with the person(s) one might be cheating on their spouse(s) with.

⊛ **compusad**; (com pyoo sad) *adj.* – emotion one might feel upon the discovery that a house they just entered has no internet connection, thus rendering their laptop a glorified MP3/DVD player. This emotion is usually doubled upon learning that such residences do have a dial-up connection.

⊛ **puntfrain**; (punt frayn) *v.* – to willingly surpress the desire to soundly kick small animals and people.

⊛ **qwykzyvx**; (kwik za vicks) *n.* – an unattractive pony even young girls would not wish for.

⊛ **bethree**; (b' 3) *adv.* – way too early.

⊛ **befive**; (b' fyv) *adv.* – the very last moment possible.

⊛ **slaphappy**; (slap hapee) *adj.* – the compulsion to physically strike another due to extreme giddiness.

SPHERICAL MAN

Wherever there is suffering
    and microwaveable food,
I'll be there.

Wherever there is injustice
    and nachos,
I'll be there.

Wherever there is crime
    near an open deli,
I'll be there.

In a world
where scrawny superheroes
will eventually fail,
the people need a man of substance
a man of true girth.

Someone who can save the world

    before dinner time.

That man is me
and I am…

…Spherical Man!

S is for Super
>as in supermarket,
>so let's go to the supermarket and buy some food
>because that would be super!

P is for Posse
>and I am my own posse.

H is for Hungry
>as in all the time,
>as in, *"Are you gonna finish that?"*

E is for Enormous.
>Everywhere you look, there I am.

R is for Rolls.
>C'mon, who doesn't like hot, buttery *rolls?*

I is for Intelligence.
>You have to be smart to know
>how to keep the weight on,
>>to know which foods are good for you and
>>which foods are good to you.

C is for Cunning
>like rewrapping Twinkies as energy bars.

A is for Attitude.
>Damn right I want it super-sized, bitch!

L is for Lurid.
 Anybody whose clothing size begins with XXX
 must be good with his mouth…

S-P-H-E-R-I-C-A-L

Look! Up in the sky, it's a moose!

 No! It's a beach ball!

  No! That's a couch!

No!
I'm Spherical Man!

 ⊛ I can leap a buffet table with a running start!
 ⊛ My cannonball is revered at every public swimming pool!
 ⊛ I'm faster than your average three-legged dog on heroin!

By day, I'm a mild-mannered Video Game Tester

By night…I'm still a mild-mannered Video Game Tester,
 only I wear an intimidating cape and
 really aggressive tights!

Join forces with me now
so we can rid the world of
Jenny Craig and her satanic cult!

We must stop Richard Simmons before
he has the whole world greased up and
wearing short-shorts!

Come together with me and
my sidekick Feedbag and
we can move toward a world
with more cushion for the pushin'.

A community where we
embrace those larger than us
knowing we may never touch fingers.

A universe where breakfast is an excuse to miss work...

ON THE PHONE: *"Hey, boss. McGee here. I woke up today
and made myself a marvelous omelet. It was much better than I
could have imagined. It put me in a great mood, and I'd really
like it to last all day, so I won't be coming to work. I'm not sick,
I'm just calling in full."*

Superman has his Kryptonite,
I have my Slim Fast,
but I am three-dimensional
and my bladder can hold far more than his;
therefore

I . . . am . . . Spherical Man!

SPHERICAL MAN AND FEEDBAG
by Dante Maddox

ARBITRARY FACTS ABOUT MIKE MCGEE, PART II

In no particular order. If you find an order, my apologies.

- 🕸 I was in the middle of a tornado in downtown Atlanta. I was having a smoke outside of a hotel, standing near a couple of other guys, when the breeze became a wind, then it became a bluster. It made me nervous. One of the gentlemen smoking near us said, in a very Georgian dialect, *"Around here, we call these a Georgia Hawk."* After a moment or two another one of the men responded with, *"You idiot, this ain't no Georgia Hawk, it's a fucking tornado."* We all then hurried into the hotel for cover. The tornado jagged its way into buildings within a ten-block radius, slamming right into CNN Headquarters. First time I ever heard of the news coming straight to them.

- 🕸 I like John Mayer, but not Jack Johnson. I recognize Jack's skill; he's just not my brand.

- 🕸 I am color blind. Specifically red-green. I see color, just not how the average person does.

- 🕸 I have deejayed at three radio stations. 1996: RFSJ - Radio Free San José, a pirate station. 1997: KSFS - San Francisco State University. 1998: KSCU - Santa Clara University. I miss radio.

- My favorite sitcoms of all time are *Roseanne, Night Court, Red Dwarf, News Radio,* and *The Office.*

- While I was born in Kentucky (and Tennessee), I have yet to return. I left a month after my birth.

- My favorite TV personalities of all time are Betty White, Johnny Carson, Bill Cosby, and Don Knotts. They are geniuses of comedy in my opinion. Especially Mrs. White.

- I have written ten screenplays. I once began writing a screenplay called *Titanic.* I had no idea James Cameron's version would come out a year later. I threw the script away. I haven't written one since I started touring in 2003. I have a new one I will write next year.

- I have a band called Monotwin. We've made lots of songs. It consists of my friend Bryce Dumont and I. We make stuff via e-mail now that he lives in England.

- I have performed live in front of over one million people in my lifetime (not including television and radio). That's not even one percent of the world.

- I smoked weed intermittently until April 5, 1995. I quit after an interesting laced experience.

🏵 I love the movie *Annie*. I've seen it more than any other film. It was a childhood favorite, along with *The Explorers* and *Spies Like Us*.

🏵 My first trip to Europe was for a show at the University of Paris (Sorbonne) with Eitan Kadosh and Derrick Brown. My last paycheck before the trip was late, so I had to go to France broke as all hell. I met Eitan and Derrick outside of the Louvre in Paris, but I could not afford to go inside. Derrick gave me shit for being broke, but helped me out along the way.

AUTHOR OUTSIDE OF THE LOUVRE (PARIS, FRANCE 2006)
Whether you have work or a job, keep money on you so you can afford to go inside the Louvre when you're already standing outside of it. At least I got a picture.

OPEN LETTER TO NEIL ARMSTRONG (FOR ITTY)

Before the world knew your name,
before it was a destination,
what was the moon like from your backyard?

5...4...3...2...1...

Dear Neil Armstrong,

I write this to you as she sleeps down the hall.
I need answers that only you might have.

When you were a boy and
space was simple science fiction,
when flying was merely a daydream
between periods of
    history
and
    physics,

    when gifts of moon dust to the one you loved
    could only be wrapped in your imagination,

your arm: strong, warm, and wrapped
across her shoulders
under her hair,

both of you gazing up
from your back porch
summers before
your distant journey.

Upon landing on the moon
as the Earth rose over the Sea of Tranquility,
did you look for her?
    What was it like to see our planet and know that
    everything you could be,
    all you could ever love and long for,

    was just floating before you?

By any chance
did you write her name in the dirt
when the cameras weren't looking?

Or maybe you surrounded both of your initials with a
    heart
for alien life to study a million years from now.

What is it like to love someone so distant?
    What words did you use to bring the moon back to
    her?
What did you promise in the moon's ear about the girl
    back home?
    Can you teach me how to fall from the sky?

I ask you these things
not because I doubt your feet/feat.
I just want to know what it's like
to go somewhere no man had ever been
only to discover she wasn't there,
    to realize your moon walk could never
    compare to the steps that lead to her.

I now know the flight home means more.

Every July I think of you.
I imagine the summer of 1969.
How lonely she must've felt while you were gone

You never went back to the moon and
I believe that's because it doesn't take rockets
to get you to where you belong.
I see that in this woman down the hall and
sometimes she seems so much further.

I'm ready for whatever steps I must take to get to her.

I've seen so many skies and
the moon always looks the same.
So I gotta say
    the rock you landed on has nothing
    on the rock of mine she's landed on.
You walked around, took samples and left.
    She's built a fire,

cleaned up the place, and
I hope she decides to stay
because on my rock
we can both breathe.

Mr. Armstrong, I don't have much.
Many times have I been upside-downtrodden
but with these empty hands
comes a heart that is full
more often than the moon.
She's becoming my world,
pulling me into orbit, and
now I know I may never find life outside of hers.

I wanna give her everything I don't have yet.
So, for her, I would go to the moon and back,
but not *without* her.
Why?
When we could claim the moon for each other with
flags made from sheets down the hall and
I'd risk it all
to kiss her under the light of Earth,
        the brightness of home.

I can do all of that and more
right here, wherever she is, and
when we gaze up
        with her arms around me,
I will not promise her gifts of
        moon dust or speeds of light.

Instead, I will gladly give her all the Earth she wants
in return for all the Earth she is,
the sound of her heartbeat and laughter
and all the time it takes
to learn to fall out the sky
in the hope that she'll catch me
cause she's one small step for a man
but she's one giant leap
for my kind.

I will do this everyday
if I can always land next to her.

MYCROPHONE

Is this thing turned on?

Cause I have a confession to make
I am more comfortable in front of a microphone
than I've ever been with a woman and
I'd love to tell you that I'm a helluva lover
but I've never loved like I would love to

On the other hand
When it's just me and a microphone

I
give
great
oral

Microphones turn me on
I am who I am at my best when
in front of a microphone

I work for the microphone
I use a microphone to my benefit
for as long as I'm on stage the mic is a part of me
I channel through it

but it's easy to get caught up

in the showmanship
to only say the words
you think people want to hear
to only write what sell books and records

Every audience has
the potential to take me higher
than I've ever been while I
force-feed the fuel that fires their fury
and the stratosphere is out of here
if the microphone's near then have no fear
cause it's

perfectly clear
that this

      po   em

is broken

What I really mean isn't being spoken
I don't wanna just say things that sound cool
They're just words that rhyme
I'm not here for the rhyme
I'd just be wasting your time

(dammit)

which is running out
and I'm not really saying anything

so here goes nothing

The microphone is a tool I use
to cram my soul into your ears
With a microphone
I can move minds and mountains
With my mouth and a microphone
my mental madness marks me more and more
Minus the microphone
many men might measure my magic
minimizing my margins
making my magnitude meager

However
Mama made me make masses
    marvel, mutter and moan
        Moaning: Michael…Matthew…McGee

Microphones magnify my mistakes
Microphones mystify my masterpieces
Microphones make my meek meanderings
    much more melodic
Microphones morph my melancholy
Microphones maneuver my massive mold
    moving my mirth merrily, merrily, merrily
Microphones make me mention my malevolence
Microphones melt my masks
Microphones manufacture myths
    making me majestic
Microphones made me Mighty Mike McGee

maybe

Then again
I'm just stringing together a bunch of words
beginning with the letter M
when in fact
the microphone is nothing without me

Sure, I can get by without a microphone
but it feels so good to be on the mic and
the only way I can describe it would be to say that:

> Stages were built so that this body would
> have a place to deliver these words
> This body was built so that
> these words could be delivered and I
> shiver at the thought of what I can do
> in front of a microphone
> I'm home up here and it's clear
> my fear is nowhere near

I wake up so you can cheer for what you hear

My ears have rung from what I've sung
My lung and tongue are raw when I'm done
My words run rings around the things I've seen and
this might sound mean,
> but the only reason I'm overweight
> is cause I don't date, skate, copulate, or fornicate

for the sake of my art
I save my energy for the herds of words
that fly like birds

I'm a big man cause I'm
packed with literary stuffing
and this is nothing
I have only just begun my run
and when my time comes
you'll know why you called me Mike

Is this thing turned on?

Cause I am

MICROPHONE AND AUDIENCE (LONGWOOD UNIVERSITY, VIRGINIA 2008)
They are there for you. They want to listen.
You better have something good to say.

ME AND MY BIG FAT MOUTH
(THE BUS STORY)

I rested bored on the harsh cloth and vinyl seat, second to last row at the back of the Greyhound bus. It was the summer of 1991; I was fifteen years old and two hundred pounds. I listened to Kool Moe Dee on cheap headphones and prayed for a stranger to consume as much of my time as possible.

The bus stopped and coolest chick of all cool chicks got on the bus alone. Her perfume preceded her entrance. I looked up to see a flash of black. Black everything: pants, boots, make-up, shirt, hair, and book bag. She was Goth I guess. I didn't know what that meant back then. But I could see that she was gorgeous.

She was a mystery on the last seat right behind me. I stalled and stalled. She was drowning out the world with her own headphones. I had to talk to her, so I hopped up and spun around to kneel on my seat, resting my chin on the top of the backrest. She looked up at me, reclined and slouched into the book she was reading. She smirked, like my presence was unusual, but my spontaneity was somewhat punk rock and welcome.

I can never remember what started the conversation, but within fifteen minutes, she had put her book and headphones away. She said she only listened to college radio—now I had to listen to college radio.

We were both fifteen, but I was the chubby class clown, she was exotic and cultured. She found very little humor in the world, but boy, could I make her laugh! Instead of having to defend myself, I was entertaining and witty. At school I used my humor to get to them before they could get to me, but this time, the more she opened up, the more I did too.

In an hour we were friends. In another half an hour we would be comfortably flirting and joking around like two people who would eventually become dorm room lovers. She thought I was funny. She thought I was special. She thought my chubby face was cute and really wanted to get to know me. This was the easiest thing I had ever done.

We were fifteen minutes away from home. We realized we lived really close to each other. It was perfect. I wanted to kiss her so badly. I knew she'd let me if I could just walk her home. We laughed and joked like old friends and when we had nothing to say, we just smiled at each other, knowing that what was happening was magical, comfortable, and delirious. It felt like we'd spent days together. We'd gone galaxies in a relationship that still had universes to build on.

She had grown so pleased with my presence that she had slowly slithered down into her seat, slouching ever more. Lying on the seat next to her she looked comfortable, but was unaware that her legs were spread and her entire pelvis was pointed right at me. I suppressed my comedic instincts. Everything was perfect. Until I joked:

"So, do you spread your legs for every guy you meet?"

Evil dread swarmed her face. At warp speed she ripped her cold book and headphones out of her bag. She opened to her dog-eared chapter and blasted The Smiths into her brain. I apologized like a cheating husband. She wouldn't look at me. I damn near cried.

In seven seconds we were strangers again, for the second time. What the fuck was I thinking? We were going to get married. We knew the chemistry between us was not normal for people our age. We were both freaks who just happened upon each other. We fit together. We saw in each other what no one else could. We found each other and I lost her.

I lost the opportunity to walk a cool chick home.

I lost my first kiss from some awesome faint black lips.

Faint because she covered her mouth every time I made her laugh, wiping away the gothic facade that first attracted me to her.

I could have fallen in love with her.

And boy, did I.

**FLOWERS CASTING RABBITS ON THE STREET
(SILICON VALLEY, CALIFORNIA 2007)**
Don't miss that chance. Everything is fleeting.

LIKE

I like you the way I like wonton
packed full of shrimp
Like too much syrup
on my pancakes…eggs…toast—and in my beard
    (accident)
Like blue whales like to say
"Hrrrreeeeeewhuuuuuuhhhwwoooaaauuuhh." (repeat 3x)

I like you a whole bunch of a lot
You're a pocketful of awesome

I like you not unlike Texans like Texas
Like fat kids like cake
Like two likes three and four likes six (five has issues)
Like tuna sandwiches like teeth
Like cherry-flavored Slurpees like
to wash down convenience store nachos
Like La-Z-Boys like Sunday afternoon asses
Like Lily likes Wilson

I like you whole bunch of a lot
    and a little bit more
You're a bottomless basket of
extra crispy French fries
    covered in awesome sauce

I like you similar to the way
pirates and frat boys like booty
Like newlyweds like Holiday Inns
Like bohemians, yuppies and Japanese like sushi
Like David Copperfield likes performing
grand scale, yet lame-ass feats of illusion
Like the U.S. Government likes performing
grand scale, yet lame-ass feats of illusion
Like testicles and homeboys like to hang
Like homeless people and break-dancers like cardboard
Like Americans like ranch dressing
Like Muppets like fisting

I like you a whole bunch of a lot and
a whole lot more times infinity, and yeah
maybe that's starting to dip into equation of love
Nevertheless, I got a thing for you
like magnets got it for refrigerators
    I'm stuck on you
    and I like it

I like you an official metric fuckload
I think you're a body full of soul and
    I hope you like me back
Even if it's like dust likes furniture
at least you're "all over me"

I'm making a pledge because I guess
I'm tired of meeting people who
define themselves by what they don't like

I just don't like that

However
I do like holding you
Like the way your pillow
holds your head when you sleep
Like gay, lesbian, transgender, transsexual,
    Irish and Mexican people hold parades
Like PBS holds fundraisers
Like the Earth holds the moon and
    the sun holds the Earth and
    how they'll constantly spin around each other forever

(I know that metaphor doesn't really make sense with
    regard to this poem because that would imply that
    there were three of us. However, that could also be
    very awesome.)

You get the idea
In my book you rock
and I like rocks

Just because I spent
    an hour or so writing this down
        doesn't mean you have to like me back
but dammit
I would really like that

RECOMMENDED SOUNDTRACKS TO SCENES IN YOUR LIFE

A few music recommendations for you to ponder, from DJ Mike McGee. Word!

⚙ Any Sigur Ros album will do when you're in the mood to write, paint, clean house, or cook. Gomez, Pavement, Squirrel Nut Zippers and R.E.M. are also good bands for these projects. New music is always a good start to a lengthy bout of creativity.

⚙ If you're in the process of cheating on someone you actually love, then you should listen to Britney Spears, 50 Cent, or Limp Bizkit, because those are what douche bags listen to. You could also listen to or watch everything Larry the Cable Guy has ever made. Your fellow frat buddies can lend these to you if you do not already have any of them in your collection. *Side note: I am very impressed that you're reading this book. Maybe those artists aren't so bad.*

⚙ If you are about to or just had a child, listen to Motown. All of it. That, and just about anything recorded between 1968 and 1974. *Let the baby hear it!*

- If you are sad, and you want to keep it going, listen to more Sigur Ros. If you are sad and you want to get happy, listen to more ska, punk, disco, Sublime, They Might Be Giants and 1980s-era pop. *Side note: Mariachi music cannot make you sad. Give it a whirl!*

- If you wish to learn from your music, consider listening to The Roots or The Tragically Hip. Side note: *One must not be a college student to listen to college radio. That shit's free!*

- Do not fear dance music! It has its place, and that place requires you to get up and shake your ass! If you like rhythm, check out some hip-hop. *Just go for it!*

- Explore music. If you're not into anything specific, grab a local paper and find a local music outlet. Discover live music. Take a risk. Take a friend. Support a new band. Try to see why others like something you might not. Get into your scene. If you don't have a scene, then get the hell out of there. Travel. See the country. Get a passport. Go to random places. Get into their environment. See why people live the way they do. Try new foods and read foreign movies. Meet a new lover. Spend real time with them. Feed them something from home. Have fun and continue traveling. Settle into a place that feels right. Be involved in your new community. Learn the lingo. Get work that pays well and provides a quality service. Appreciate the past, but look ahead. Enjoy all of this and remember it often. Do not allow yourself to listen to music simply because it's from your high school era. It'll always be there. Familiarity is wonderful, but variety is fantastic.

Side note: Pay for this music when you can. Aside from your opinion, they are still artists.

IN SEARCH OF MIDNIGHT

Somewhere in the cold midnight of Idaho
two women prepare to leave town together
they're tired of drawing public attention to
the way they hold each other's hands

    (Couples in Idaho do hold hands, they just don't
    usually look like two women)

So they hit the road for California
where people still segregate themselves from each other
and every city's East Side is feared by suburbanites
because the local news anchor hates the East Side
so he reminds us
every night on the nightly news
just how dangerous it is with
all of its minorities and crime

He prefers downtown at midnight
where he can afford to be a teenager again
and maybe even on top of one

Somewhere on the East Side of Vancouver, British Columbia
a fourteen-year-old woman
hops on a bus to get to Hastings Street, downtown
where her body is worth a little bit more
she wonders if any girl has ever

taken their pimp to the school prom and
watches out for all the hookers who are younger than her
dead mothers cannot question a child who sleeps through
    the afternoon

When she has enough money
she'll catch a bus to Montreal or Toronto
and dance for the rest of her life
    but currently
    it is midnight
    and she has rent to make

At midnight in Hollywood, there are waiters and
    waitresses practicing their Academy Award acceptance
    speeches while serving you chicken wings and hash
    browns

At midnight in Denver, there are poets heating up their
    dinners on radiators and washing their clothes by hand
    cause quarters are saved for buses and homeless people

At midnight in San Antonio, a man holds a party because
    the body warmth will heat up his house just long
    enough for him to get a few hours of sleep before
    teaching his elementary school class in the morning

At midnight in Portland, a college student sleeps in
    someone else's bed every night just so she can continue
    her education

At midnight in Seattle, a man hears a poem that might
keep him alive for one more day

At midnight in San Diego, an illegal immigrant puts
American cash in an envelope to be mailed back to his
family in Mexico, while eating his first Big Mac on his
late night lunch break

At midnight in Oklahoma City, a young girl gets drunk
for the first time and realizes it is the best thing to do
because it is the only thing to do

At midnight in Chicago, a man sits in jail for the first time
in his life, for a crime he did not commit. He knows
nobody will believe him because he knows all too well
the color of his own skin. He marvels at how far we've
come

At midnight in some of the worst parts of Detroit, a
woman prays to her God for the first time in years
because of something she heard on the news

She really wants tomorrow to be a better day

At midnight in San José, a fat man puts more food into his
mouth to try to feel better about the world or forget it
all together

At midnight throughout the rest of the world, people are
exactly who they should be

They are you

You are quite possibly someone you'll never share with
    anyone else

You're the one who could leave hot food
at the feet of sleeping homeless people
then worry about your next meal when no one is looking

You're the one who may never function at noon
the one who everyone will believe
left the planet just a little too soon

You might not have tongues
    but you have so much to say

I know, I've heard you

You are doing what it takes
    to stay sane and alive
you are not wearing the finest clothes
you are online and searching
you are making free calls on phones you cannot afford
you are reaching out to yourself
in an attempt to find perfection

    whether it is within yourself or in someone else

Somewhere out there

it must exist
it must be possible to achieve
what we all want
because if it isn't
then midnight comes to us for no reason
we start over every day for no reason
there must be something perfect in this world
and I believe it comes to us all
at midnight

REDWOOD FOREST (BIG BASIN, CALIFORNIA 2005)
Up is always a good place to look.

I'M NOT…BUT IF I WERE

I'm not thin…but if I were…
I'd be the thinnest man this side of the NBA.
I'd wake up each morning with a smile on my face
and I'd sing songs in the shower by Skinny Puppy and
　　　Thin Lizzie
as I lathered up into an emaciated frenzy.
I'd be thinner than thin.
I'd wear a skinny tie to work and drink decaffeinated coffee
　　　with soy milk.
I would be a thin bastard!
No! I would be the *thinnest* bastard,
looking for other thin bastards to give a bony handshake to.

Me and my thinness would travel the world around
spreading joy and celery and
I would call up Brad Pitt
just to say, *"You've put on some weight!"*

The world would love me if I were thin and
they'd want to be thin right along with me.
I'd teach them all how to be thin with my thin handbook.
We'd do thin things and eat thin things, while going to
　　　thin places and
when one of us saw something we liked, we'd get the
　　　skinny on it!

But I'm not thin.
I've been hit on by more overweight people than I have
    thin people.
Maybe they know something I don't.
But for now, I don't need to be thin
and I'm cool with anyone who is.

I'm also not gay…but if I were…
I'd be the gayest man this side of San Francisco.
I'd wake up each morning with a smile on my face
and I'd sing show-tunes in the shower
as I lathered up into a homosexual frenzy.
I'd be gayer than gay!
I'd wear a rainbow tie to work and drink coffee with my
    pinky out.
It would be a gay pinky!
No! It would be the *gayest* pinky,
looking for other gay pinkies to give hand jobs to!

Me and my gayness would travel the world around
spreading joy and condoms,
and I would call up Brad Pitt
just to say, *"Come OUT and play!"*

The world would love me if I were gay and
they'd want to be gay right along with me.
I'd teach them all how to be gay with my gay handbook.
We'd do gay things and eat gay things while going to gay
    places and
when one of us saw something we liked, we'd say, *"That is so gay!"*

But I'm not gay.
I've been hit on by more gay men than I have straight women.
Maybe they know something I don't.
But for now, I don't need to be gay
and I'm cool with anyone who is.

I am, however, Mike McGee...
and because of this I am the best Mike McGee I know.
I wake up most mornings with drool on my face
and I sing my own songs in the shower as I lather up into
    a Mike McGee frenzy.
I'm Miker than Mike!
I don't wear a tie to work and I like coffee
but
fuck latte, fuck half-caff, fuck Starbucks, fuck you, fuck me,
which rhymes well with Mike McGee.

Me and my Mike McGee-ness should travel the world around
spreading joy and sugar-free pudding
and I would call up Brad Pitt
just to say, *"Holy shit! You answered!"*

The world doesn't have to love Mike McGee and no one
    wants to be Mike McGee with me, but I could teach
    you all how to be me with
my Mike McGee Handbook and we would
do Mike things and eat Mike things
while we're at my house, and
when one of us saw something we liked, we'd say, *"Smell it!"*

I am Mike McGee and I've never been hit on by Mike
    McGee.
Maybe I know something I don't,
but for now I don't want to be anybody else
cause I'm pretty fucking cool with Mike McGee.

Smell it!

BMX
(FOR JAMIE)

On Christmas Day 1982, I got a black BMX bike. I was six years old and it was the first time in my life I had something that everyone on the block wanted—even the girls wanted one. I don't think Santa Claus realized what he had given me. Earth knows I never could have asked my mom for one. They were so expensive and money was so tight, but I was more than happy to accept it.

I would ride around in circles up and down my street whether I wanted to or not because I didn't know how and when to kick the pedals back to apply the brake. I would ride down the street, then slow down, and gently crash into the next available parked car.

By Spring of 1983, I had mastered my bike and its brakes. My little brother Jamie, a full year and a half younger than me, had gotten a banana seat Huffy the same Christmas morning from the same Santa Claus that had blessed me with my machine; we were Ponch and Jon straight out of the TV show CHiPs, riding side by side, scream-humming the theme song as if the cameras were rolling, going 55 mph down some stretch of freeway in L.A.

"Da-Da, DaDa-Da!"

We never caught any bad guys. Did Ponch and Jon ever catch any? Seemed like they only saved children from runaway buses, so that's what Jamie and I did.

In two years we must have saved about three thousand invisible kids from certain doom on California's treacherous highways. Roads we never knew the names of, but always seemed to look like our street, and when one of us had a flat, or a loose chain, so did the other, to be fair. It was an unwritten rule between my brother and me. If I didn't have a bike, neither did he. Without our bikes, I became Starsky and he became Hutch, or we were the Dukes of Hazzard, and the mission of our episode was to track down a tire pump so that we could become Ponch and Jon again to save more invisible children together.

Over the years we realized how much we needed our bikes and that we could do very little without them. If mom needed a gallon of milk, we both went to the store—even though it was a one-person job. One of us had to watch out for spies and bad guys, or runaway buses, while the other one carried the "secret special" milk in his backpack.

When I came back home in 1985 after living with our dad for three months, Jamie explained how he had been waiting for me so that he could ride his bike. *Jamie had waited to ride his bike for three months.*

For the next couple of years we rode the wind, ever stretching our boundaries and pushing the limits of how far Mom would let us ride. We would ride by and laugh at the younger kids still break-dancing in 1987, yet, we were still Ponch and Jon deep down inside, and even though we had stopped saving invisible children, we were always on the lookout for runaway buses.

Our bikes began to serve greater purposes, but at different times and in different ways, to where I hardly ever saw Jamie and my BMX wasn't as cool anymore. It was a burden. When I'd get home from a long ride from the store for milk—alone—I'd just toss my bike on the lawn, and sometimes I'd leave it there overnight because I just didn't give a shit anymore. Ponch was helpless all by himself.

Then one beautiful summer afternoon, after a quick candy run to nearby Dick's Market, I tossed my bike on the lawn one last time. My mom then asked me to go back to the store. I took her money and headed back outside, but my bike was gone. My childhood disappeared in ten minutes. So Jamie walked with me to the store and we laughed and joked and forgot about what Ponch and Jon rode, concentrating on what they meant to each other.

We had saved so many invisible children together. I cannot count how many times our mother had to scream for us down the street to come eat dinner…all because of Santa Claus and his glorious gift-giving judgment. No matter how many times we moved, we were together with our bikes.

No present after that Christmas ever seemed to come close to our bikes. Every time we got home late, mom never seemed upset. It wasn't until after I lost my bike that I realized that my mom's handwriting on the Christmas tags matched Santa's letter for letter. She was the reason we were always late for dinner and she didn't actually mind as long as Ponch was watching over Jon.

When I lost my bike, Jamie didn't ride his anymore. It sat and got rusty in our backyard, then it just seemed to fade away. Since then, Jamie and I haven't needed a bike to hang out. We get along just fine, wherever we are or wherever we're going, no matter what vehicle gets us there.

Even if they are runaway buses.

THE SMILE

I'm sitting in the break room at work. Just outside the door is a window to the street. Anybody who walks by said window can see me in said break room.

As I ate my toasted Asiago bagel with cream cheese, I lamented the fact that I had to return to work. Outside of the break room were grumpy-ass customers just waiting to yell at me and my nametag.

I continued eating when this woman walked by the window, made eye contact with me and smiled. Not a "what're you looking at" type of smile, more like: "Hey there sad eyes, take this smile from my lips. Let not this day bring you darkness, but a new light and harmony. Let thy peace be done."

It was a shine-on-you-crazy-diamond kind of smile

I was awestruck by her power; she went by at the speed of modern humanity. It would have been easy to miss her noble gift as she passed me by. Her being a stranger, I assumed she could only smile at chubby white men with bagel crumbs in their goatees. It is possible, however, that when our eyes met, she farted.

But that singular smile was salvation from a seemingly sucky day. Like a virus, she passed to me this simple contagion of contortion.

My face was paralyzed into a position of positivity. A smile so solid, you'd swear I lost my virginity in the break room twice to Milla Jovovich wearing nothing but Scotch tape. This was beyond sexual bliss, this was me being giddy on a Monday at work thanks to a stranger on the street. She compelled me to pass on a smile doubly-wide to everyone who came before me. I left with my coworkers smiling like they'd just won a year's supply of cake, milk, and weed. There I was, this giddy, pear-shaped genius, smiling so hardcore my gums were bleeding. My mission of mouth mechanics had me making mad men merry, while working wildly to wow women to wonder, "Why the fuck is he so happy?" and "How do men that chubby get so damn cute?"

I'll tell you how!

Smiling is sexy, and I smile all the time. I am cute because I still believe smiling is the first step we can take toward helping out one person at a time. Even if I didn't have teeth, I'd still smile, because teeth are an unimportant aesthetic in the diplomacy of smiling. It's almost better than eating a free buffet dinner with a stripper at a casino where you just won three hundred bucks on a silver dollar you found in the gutter.

Almost.

Abraham Lincoln didn't smile and look at what happened to him.

Smiles are the last proof and truth that we are

beautiful, that we can do more than we believe ourselves capable. A complete stranger smiled at me, and although my life didn't attain perfection, it did get a little better. It's as if she said, "Baby, I know how you feel, and we'll get through this."

Her smile carried me through my day and later that afternoon I stepped into a coffee shop where I usually buy orange juice, but instead, I asked the girl behind the counter if she would have dinner with me sometime. She said and nodded yes, punctuating it with a smile. It caused a revelation to smile across my brain as I realized I had never asked a woman out before and that made me smile.

ALL SMILES (SOME HOTEL, SOMEWHERE ELSE 2008)
Smile whenever the feeling strikes you.

EVERY DAY
(FOR ITTY)

Every day I rewrite her name across my chest
so that those who wish to break my heart
will know who to answer to later

A name to the ass-kicking
if you will

She has no idea that I've taught my tongue to make pennies
and if only our mouths would meet
I would slip one to the back of her throat and
make a wish for more meetings like that

I wish
that someday
my head on her belly might look like home
like doubt-to-doubt resuscitation
because time is supposed to mean more than skin

She doesn't know that I have taught my arms to close
    around her clocks
so they can withstand the fallout from her autumn

She is so explosive that
volcanoes watch her and learn
Terrorists want to strap her to their chests

because she is a cause worth
dying next to

Time has taught me to pick up her pieces
put her back together
so she can be sure
to fall apart again
down the road

Lady, let's catch the next tornado home
    Let's plant cantaloupe trees in our backyard
    then I'll remind you:
        I don't like cantaloupe
        and they certainly don't grow on trees

We can laugh about this
and how you can
make flawed look so beautiful

The word smitten
    is to how I feel about you
What a kiss
    is to romance
So maybe my lips to yours
could be the penance to this confession
because I am the only one
preaching your defunct religion
sitting alone at your altar
praising you out of faith

I am teaching the congregation
about the miracles
you've committed to survival
through bad choices
between keeping your friends at a distance
    and sleeping with your enemies

I probably shouldn't be so ready
to pull out the nails
you hammer in every morning
once you realize he's not coming back

You cannot do this hard-knock life alone

You are all the softness
a rock dreams of being
the mistakes the rain makes
at picnics
    but I packed this basket
    so I will sit here
    with you, drenched

I will gladly
take on your ocean
just to swim beneath you
so I can kiss the bends of your knees
in appreciation for the work they do
keeping your head above water

DIRTY DIMES

I know how unnoticeable I am
in my new uniform
My appearance must seem so uncaring

Right now I am one of three people
wearing a tie at 11 p.m.
in San José, California

I'm four days and three-eighths into
my new graveyard shift at
one of America's super-drugstores

Those that use my services at night know
they can only come out when the rest of civilization
has laid its head to dream of newer
crisper fifty-dollar bills
maybe even hundreds

I really don't care

They can put the aroma of a new car in a bottle
why not that new money smell in an aerosol can
I know I'll already reek of cash when I get home
I just won't have any of my own

but I really don't care

Retail's a whore that never sleeps
constantly screwing everyone that comes in for one kiss
and I'm her pimp, selling off everything she has
and everything she is

Aisle number three is full of Easter candy
like a pink and blue bunker of war
only the soldiers here are children
armed with cap guns and silly string
or I at least assume they are
because I'm sure I'm asleep
when it all takes place

This job is bullshit
whether I'm flipping burgers
or telemarketing some cheap, toxic product
It's all the same
It's not what I want
or should be doing

My new boss watches me intently
she follows behind me and
rearranges things I place incorrectly
I am three years old again
and I could get used to it

My new uniform fits me like a
condom on a vagina
or a straight jacket on a snake

at least it's comfortable
I suppose I could get used to this

My boss has been here for at least three years
I've never held a job for that long
I don't think I could ever devote that much time
to someone else's money
it is my money too
even though it makes me feel weird
it's still my money that I'm earning
I sweat for that paycheck every two weeks
maybe someday
one of them might set me free

One-tenth of the money I put into that cash register is mine
so I count each and every customer that comes in
It's not an exact science
but it keeps me sane and sweating
and this is when I start to care

I count the customers in tens
every tenth customer is responsible for my paycheck
it's easier to put a random face to it all
whatever it is they purchase
they get it from me
    from my sweat
    from my aching feet
    from my eight hours on the clock and
    my three hours on the bus

My seventh customer makes a line at my register
with nothing in hand but a wad
of money that smells like gratuity
he's a brawny bastard who
looks like he just woke up from
a respectful nap
he asks for
instant film at 1:46 a.m.
he doesn't want a stranger
developing his pictures
he drives a cab the same time I clean this store
most of his passengers
are inebriated, lonely women
who want nothing more than
anonymous backseat coitus and a ride home
they probably regret paying this man
because for him
it's all profit

He shows me pictures of his models
Large-breasted thirty- and forty-somethings
sprawled out on the hood of his cab
looking drunk, horny and married

The nipples in the photos are clearer
than my thoughts on the actual situation
I asked to see them and now I regret it
these ladies probably have
children I went to school with

I really don't care

Twenty minutes later
customer eight rings my bell
and I "rush" to the counter
I smile inside because she is a beautiful woman
and what would a woman this gorgeous
be doing in my store at 2 a.m.
her basket of groceries does two things:
    ⚡ it immediately answers my question
    ⚡ and it gives her a future
or at least a Saturday night
one that won't be alone
because condoms are something you buy
before you need them

Just in case

She must know the man she's meeting up with
unless large condoms are
a safe assumption between strangers
Maybe she's getting a ride from that cab driver
but it is my hopeful assumption that she
is too young and too pretty for his portfolio

I ring her up
she pulls out her checkbook
I want to laugh at her
because she's in such a rush
but has decided to make her
purchase with the slowest form

of payment known to man
so I take my sweet time
filling out the information
from her driver's license
she never makes eye contact with me
she knows I know and
I'm the only thing in her way

Men on their way to sex can laugh
and brag with the cashier
 Women get nervous and think
  everyone knows what they're about to do
But I just don't care

Customer nine makes her way to my register
she's a tired mother who works late
and is probably raising her kids alone
She seems proud even though
she still has her Denny's apron on
Her name tag says "Tina"
then "Old Maid" underneath it
in invisible ink
I see it
 and she wears it well

All I am is the guy who rings up her
bleach, detergent, toothpaste, milk,
cereal and children's cough medicine
I feel sorry for her kid
I hate being sick
but I really don't care

She takes her change and leaves with a smile
Honestly, I hope I helped put it there

I go back to aisle three
to continue its reconstruction
destroyed by daytime warfare
starring cowboys and indians
carelessness and capitalism
I get paid to lie

The door chime rings
I hear two women enter the store
they sound amused and hurried
I work on the shelf in front of me and
wait for the bell on the counter
They are customer number ten
their money is mine and they'll never know
they personally helped me pay rent

I am eager to meet them

Once they've completed their shopping
they ring the bell on the counter
I glide past the peanut brittle and crayons
and turn toward the cash register
where I see two women
barely thirty
looking for me
while waiting patiently for my slow legs to reach them

My eyes are drawn to the counter
    then to the items they are buying
        then to the skin of the woman closest to me

She's wearing a man's dress shirt
completely unbuttoned and no bra
the skin I see is her stomach and her chest
I can see her entire right breast
so I look away, ashamed
I am forced to look at her face
which is far too thin to be healthy

A bandana squeezes her bald head tightly
her eyes bulge like surprise
her sunken face looks like that of a former beauty queen

She stares at the products as I ring them up
and I try not to stare at her small breasts
every time her shirt swings open

Her friend stands behind her
clean and strong
    maybe she's her lover
    maybe they're related
none of the items I ring up
tell me who this other woman is
they only say that the exposed woman is very ill
and bleeds from sores, wounds
that she is contagious
she is afflicted with something

These products have no brand names
so she is poor
they are poor together and
ready to give me their money

She must have cancer
I want to strike up a conversation
something to get my mind away from this
apparent mortality

Maybe she has AIDS
maybe she shared the wrong needle
with the wrong person
but every dying human
looks like a junkie at some point

Her friend looks at her with worry
cementing all my assumptions
      she is her guardian
            the one who will watch and is watching her die
            the one who will pick out her cheap coffin
            the only one willing to bury her

There is so much love between these two

I am taking up way too much of their precious time
so I speed up the process and bag their stuff as quickly
as possible

I hit the total button: Three dollars and sixty-seven cents
in low-grade medical supplies

In all of my methods of maintaining sanity
these items are mine and they are Customer Ten
maybe these items will help her live another day
I should just give them to her
but that would draw attention
I would be another man
reminding a living woman that she is dying

Even justice sleeps sometimes

The friend pulls out some money
the dead woman beats her to the counter
with a handful of dimes
    dirty dimes
the kind collected in a cup on a street corner
downtown dimes discarded by uptown business men and
women who aren't dying this very minute

    If everything would just freeze before me
    I could let loose and cry and not disturb their shopping
    experience
    but inside me
    in a place people rarely visit in public situations
    my heart's feeling picket signs
    being held up by my guts that read

    let them see how
    you feel right now

    and

you're just jealous
cause she gets to leave

Back in the real world
my pity turns to anger as she picks lint
out of the change on the counter
I am upset that this nice woman is so ill
    but she's cracking smiles at me
    with big teeth through thin lips
she knows I know
she may be content
but I don't want her to be a stranger anymore

I watch her count the dimes
off the counter and into her bony little hand

I try not to count along with her
but deep down
I truly hope she comes up short
the feeling is so strong
I'm sure I will forever regret
not saying it aloud

I take thirty-six dimes and try to assume some sort of apathy
but it never works
these women leave with smiles on their faces
that I couldn't have possibly given them

For the rest of the night
I can't focus on shit
but I make sure every customer after them

gets a dirty dime in their change and
I try not to cry
because this job doesn't pay me
for that sort of thing

It is 3 a.m. and I am tired
of trying not to care about people who don't know me

TRUTH IN ADVERTISING (CHICAGO, ILLINOIS 2007)
If only all corporations implemented more honesty on the job.

TONIGHT
(FOR MARANDA)

Tonight the moon is a
mere sliver of what it could be
and I'm twice what I have been and
if you're just you
then us three are a fantastic crowd of two
especially tonight
    just us together

You are a heavy, weird scarf
you are way too much
and I want more

I love your arms around my neck
your eyes so close, just holding mine
I wanna hold you in return
like an apple holds its seeds
Go ahead
Grow out of me you hairy tree

If I could live on your tongue
I'd dodge the words you use to express yourself
then I'd scramble to the edge of your teeth
to watch them fly and
when the right word came along
I would grab onto it
and fly out

becoming part of your expression
your verbal essence

I hope you don't mind me telling the world that you love
    me right
that when you love me
I get all slip-shiny and pitch-perfect

Only, when you're gone
I become half of what I could be
then I just wanna sleep all day
because sleeping is this grand roulette
We close our eyes
just hoping they'll open

I can love you so much better in my dreams
I can wipe away your tears with a giraffe and
it would make you laugh and
then we'd get naked and ride a train for no good reason
to Omaha, Nebraska and
even though we don't live in Omaha, Nebraska
in my dreams
as long as you're there
it feels like home

in real life
in your scarfy arms
it feels like home

But if tonight turns out to be a dream
know this
    I still love only you

I add nothing to you and take nothing away
my dreams keep you the way you are
    except sometimes there's two of you and
    for some reason
    I'm dressed like Jean Luc Picard and

we ride that giraffe to the horizon
then we wait together
for home to arrive

THE HORIZON (HONOLULU, HAWAII 2008)
The night is always on its way. It'll be okay. I'll wait with you.

PEOPLE ARE UGLY WHEN I'M SAD

Today, in a nauseous state of spontaneous sadness and confusion, I stood alone on a street corner and considered stepping into oncoming traffic.

It was half a minute of serious thought.

The conclusion I came to was that my level of trust in California drivers is much higher than I had previously considered. The cars on the road would've probably stopped just in time and the initial result would've been a chaotic moment of stalled cars and yelling.

But it is that yelling that would have made it all worth it.

"Get out of the road, jerkbowl!"

In New York, although it is not my home, I am confident that the statement would've been followed by fat-ass, fucker, or asshole. Fat-ass is my favorite, because it is true and I live for honesty.

Instead of causing this scene, I crushed out my cigarette, returned to my outdoor coffee shop table, enjoyed the strong last sip of mocha and watched beautiful people smile in the sun.

I'm glad I decided to live today.

JOY (IMAGE BY J. MEDYNSKI), (VANCOUVER, B.C. 2006)
Sadness is not a friend, it is a tool. Welcome it, but work
toward sending it away once it's run its course.

INSTRUCTIONS FOR A SEVENTEEN-YEAR-OLD BOY

Boy,

The world will not allow
you to know everything,
but you can listen to the one you love.
She has a strength
that cannot be measured in weight,
but in time,
and if you're the right one,
her hands will turn to locks around yours.
She won't let go

Forever will make more sense
but not all of the sense.

Remember:
she is built of u-turns
boomerang wood,
and the softest softness,
like invisible cotton
caught in a breeze
from the mouths of holy ghosts
and gods that only know
temptation and suffering.
They will teach you
the in-betweens of

Saturdays and Sundays,
the feeling of never getting out of bed,
and finding the effort
to do nothing together.

Cook for her,
make her laugh,
and dance with her
every time she asks (duh).

All we ever want is
a million dollars,
soft sheets,
and a twenty-eight-hour Saturday
    in bed with her
    and no phone calls.

We can't afford any of it
and rarely notice
once we've earned
even one of them.

But if you do earn it,
tell the world about it,
but understand
that they will want
to learn it for themselves
probably just like you do right now.

SPORADIC FACTS ABOUT MIKE MCGEE, PART III

An unparticular order.

- 🎞 In 1983 or 1984, on a trip to Universal Studios, I saw the production crew, Delorean, and clock tower set for *Back to the Future* during a break in shooting.

- 🎞 In October or November of 1985, I woke from spinal surgery paralyzed from the waist down. I regained use of my legs through three weeks of physical therapy. It is the most pain I've ever experienced. As I began to feel my legs again, it caused an extreme pins and needles effect from the waist down. Only morphine made it bearable.

- 🎞 My favorite foods, in this order, are seafood/sushi (absolutely any kind), soup (any kind), Mexican, and Indian. Throw 'em all in a pan, bake it, and call it McGeeserole.

- 🎞 I have never seen the films *Top Gun, Chasing Amy,* or *Annie Hall.* It's almost a challenge now to not see them.

- 🎞 I find most anime completely uninteresting.

- 🎞 I love to dance. I thoroughly enjoy trance, hip-hop, house, techno, and drum & bass when I am dancing. I probably look like an idiot doing it, but

I don't care. However, I do not like Top 40-style dance clubs. I prefer dive bars, weddings, and parties as places of dance.

⊛ I am slightly: aglophobic (pain), talassophobic (ocean/sea), agoraphobic (open space, crowds), antlophobic (floods), and astrophobic (outer space). I love the sky and outer space, but being in them is unsettling.

⊛ I have a knack for remembering people's names and faces, and this is because I felt so forgettable as a child. I realized that if I took the time to remember someone's name, they would be grateful. I always felt so grateful when someone remembered my name, so I made it a life-long duty of mine to make people happy in this way. It pains me and leads me to feelings of extreme guilt when I meet someone a second, third or fourth time and still have yet to lock in their name. I will ask them again, of course, but I will feel horrible for having to do so. I will not lie my way to figuring out a name, but the more people I meet, the harder it gets.

PORTRAIT OF AUTHOR AT THE HOLLYWOOD WALK OF FAME (HOLLYWOOD, CALIFORNIA 2006)
Be true to yourself. Others will appreciate it.
My love of Phil Collins is already changing the world.

GOING YOUNG

When a child considers death, it is not a quick, passing thought. There must be a course in medical school that teaches doctors and nurses how to tell a person they're going to die, let alone a child.

When I was a child, I had certain medical annoyances that sent me to the hospital pretty often. The year I was born, I was diagnosed with Spina Bifida, a birth defect that ranges in severity with each patient, but most cases are far more serious than mine.

In 1985, at nine years old, I lived in the children's ward at Walter Reed Memorial Hospital in Washington D.C. I met a nurse from Texas. He was in his mid-twenties, six-foot-something, black, and nothing like any of the hundreds of nurses I had met before him. He would change my diaper, feed me, bathe me, and hold my hand when the doctors needed more blood from my already tapped veins. His voice was outstanding and it would boom when he got mad, but that only happened once, and I'll get to that later.

One of my greatest regrets in life has always been that I cannot remember this nurse's name. I remember everything else about him, and have done my best to try to remember all other names since. However, his name isn't as important as his voice. His voice was built from singing—choirs, choruses, and just spontaneous songs for all the kids at Walter Reed Memorial Hospital in Washington D.C. This man always seemed to do what was right, no matter how it looked or sounded; if it felt right to him, then it had to be done.

He laughed at my jokes and said he couldn't wait to see me on TV someday, because he knew I'd make it out of there. I was only nine years old, and maybe he said the same thing to all of the other kids in my ward, but he sure made me feel like I was one-of-a-kind. He encouraged me to be funny and broaden my skills. He devoted most of his time to the kids that weren't going make it out—all the ones lying in their last beds. He would sing for them all the time and just sit near them when they slept, so that they would have him to wake up to, the next best thing to mom and dad.

Sometimes, I would get jealous because he was my only friend, and yet I had to share him with the other kids. Most of my peers were my age, but had little, bald heads and weighed half of what I did. When I asked my friend why they looked this way he said, "Cause they're special. They get to go home early."

I knew what he meant; at the time, I was a devout Catholic with no fear of heaven, but my friend assured me that the one thing he had to look forward to every day was a certain sense of fear from all of those kids. So, to get away from the torture of chemo, radiation, tests—and the fact that most of their siblings didn't come to visit cause it was just too hard to bear seeing them that way—these kids would get away from it all by going to the children's playroom. It was room full of every toy and game imaginable, donated by the healthy children of all the doctors and nurses of Walter Reed Memorial Hospital in Washington D.C.

Personally, I avoided the children's playroom.

Then one beautiful day, my friend came in just to check on me. I was alone in my room, and he asked where the other kids were, and I said they had all gone to the playroom. He asked me why I hadn't gone with them and I said, "Cause it's depressing." He stared at me for some time then said, "No, *that's* depressing." He said, "You got something these kids don't. A future. These kids are gonna get all their birthday presents early, just in case. You make all the nurses laugh, but you don't share it with the people who need it, and that ain't right." His voice boomed like never before. He was so mad at me. He left the room and I didn't see him for three days, which is impossible in a hospital. I stayed in my bed that whole time, wondering if he would ever come back. When he did, he came armed with a wheelchair, and without saying a word he put me in it and wheeled me down to the playroom.

I sat before a room full of the most destroyed children I'd ever seen—kids that should be adults right now. My friend leaned into me and whispered, "Please, make them smile. I know you can do it." Then he announced to the crowd of bald kids that I had come to perform for them. They all turned to face me and waited.

My friend the nurse left the room and listened down the hall. All of the children at Walter Reed Memorial Hospital who weren't bedridden were there. I can say with assurance that they did smile, the whole room smiled and laughed at everything I did. The entire hospital could feel the energy from those kids. They enjoyed themselves like there was a tomorrow. I can't remember anything I said or did, but there is nothing in the world better than a room full of the happiest children in the world, children who have every reason not to smile or laugh, or enjoy themselves. Some of them smiled for the last time.

My nurse was right, and that day, I discovered who I wanted to be. That was my first audience ever and it was surely the most important audience I will ever have.

OF DIAMONDS AND MEN
(FOR LIZA)

As the dark blue blanket burns toward brightness
a woman sleeps
content
but curious as to where her life is headed

South of her
in a different city
is a man who has not been able to put to rest
the mental images of this young
beautiful woman
sleeping north of him

She comes to him throughout his day
in the breaking stillness of a smile

This man thinks of diamonds
   the more flawed a diamond is
   the less it is worth

If people were valued like diamonds
what would we hold onto?

Unlike diamonds
he feels he would rather have the radiance of her flaws
than the darkness of her absence

In the past
he felt his life like that of sad zirconium
shaped like a diamond
with the appearance of a diamond
but flawed from the start
destined to remain flawed
never a chance to shine

But this woman north of him
sleeping soundly
makes this man south of her
feel like a thirty-three carat gem
shining not unlike that of the most brilliant sun
    a dot of pure light in an empty sky
    a diamond so flawed
    it's perfect
and no one else seems to notice

She gives this man new reason
to feel like something so wonderful
it should only be shared with her
sleeping soundly
just north of him
in an entirely different city
underneath the same changing sky

STREETLIGHT (VANCOUVER, BRITISH COLUMBIA 2005)
I sat under a streetlight and realized that there is darkness
to protect us from things we should not see. The night is ugly
so the day can be beautiful.

FOR THE BIRDS (AT 3:33 AM)

I sat out on her balcony, the dawn, waiting.
There was a bird sitting near the table.
It seemed to be comfortable with my presence.

Maybe it fell.
Maybe it was just waiting to die.

Tears dropped over my cigarette
and the bird seemed to listen.

I stalled on words that just wouldn't come out at 3:00am
   words for the bird
    words for her.

Deep down I know
I too have fallen and I am just just waiting to die.

Joy comes when she sleeps.
I'm ready to tell her everything.
Three cups of coffee in me—a thousand words later

I am with her in sleep.
She seems to be comfortable with my presence, wounded,
waiting,
not sure how to fly.

'STACHED AWAY (SILICON VALLEY 2007)
I was aiming for a Sam Elliot 'stache, but due to chubbiness,
I ended up with a Wilford Brimley.

LAYABOUT

Let's lay in a graveyard
    six feet above all of them
    who have lived their lives
    to the exact fullest

Let's lay like them
    with our eyes to the sky and
    our backs turned
    against the world

SHOULDA
(FOR MAUREEN)

I like some of my smaller regrets
They sit like little security alarms
in the back of my head
going off when I'm close to
making the same mistakes

There is one alarm
that goes off from time to time
before I sleep and
it wakes me up to the day ahead
this alarm is one I will call
    "I Should Have Kissed You At The Eiffel Tower"
because I am a poet
and really should not have
missed that chance
before I left Paris

That specific regret
reminds me every day
how lonely the day ahead will be without you
It is a constant regret
that I will never forget as long as I live
and if I could get back to the
number of moments that could have
been made up of our mouths' meeting

like the handshake of two countries
swearing to a treaty of love
    not out of war
    but out of a greater peace
    a union that erases borders like
    rain to sidewalk chalk
I would do it faster than Yes

Regret shouldn't be the act of hop-scotching over
    what should have been

What could have been our first kiss was
amiss only because I was scared of
actually being in the presence of the right girl
and there is no question why we were
put near each other for that short period of time
from such a marvelous distance

    No
    the only question is
    why we didn't act

IN-SEINE (PARIS, FRANCE 2005)
I'd rather have had the balls to kiss her than to have taken this picture.

SIMPLE TRUTHS

1. Don't hit your kids
⊕ Hitting your children makes them angry
⊕ Angry children become lawyers who rob defenseless old ladies of their social security

So don't hit your kids
or they'll force old people to eat cat food

2. Don't play hooky
⊕ Playing hooky from school leaves you with nothing to do throughout the day
⊕ You'll walk the streets looking for things to help pass the time

So don't play hooky
or someone will offer you money for sex

3. Don't start smoking
⊕ Smoking is expensive
⊕ Cigarettes are catching up in street value
⊕ If you'll buy cigarettes from strangers, you'll buy anything

So don't start smoking
or you'll have crack babies

4. Eat your vegetables

⊛ Vegetables give us energy
⊛ If you have no energy, you'll grow up lazy
⊛ Lazy people don't go to stores to buy condoms on their way to sex

So eat your vegetables
or you'll get a sexually transmitted disease

THE KISS
(FOR KNOWLES)

The first night I lay
next to her
I was on my belly
She lifted my shirt and
saw my scars

I had told her about them
    that they were some of my
greatest achievements
and so she kissed them
as if they were
hers

I knew then
I would always
have love
in my heart
for this woman
    whose scars
    outstretched mine
    without being seen

This never stopped me
from trying to kiss them
too

Trying to heal them
with lips and ears
and whole lot of my time

WORK EXPERIENCE

Mike McGee
Silicon Valley, California
www.mikemcgee.net

OBJECTIVE
⊛ To pay rent and not feel like a slacker.

PERSONAL NOTES
⊛ I believe work is a very good thing, but jobs always suck.
⊛ I will surf your internet.
⊛ Employment gaps = unemployment = my most creative periods.

SKILLS
I excel at conversation. I can answer any phone. I have an above-average knowledge of computers, people and communication. I respect those who respect me. I like helping and learning. I despise selling things to people who have a habit of buying things they don't need.

WORK EXPERIENCE
McDonald's; *Everything*
OCTOBER 1993 – JUNE 1995

Some of my fondest employment memories are

from this McDonald's. My good friend John Heindel was a supervisor and put in a good word for me. I was hired at $4.50 an hour! This was real money.

I got hired to close the store at 11 p.m. We would lock the doors at 10:58, turn up the radio, light up cigarettes, and start cleaning. We'd drink shakes and sodas, and eat up the burgers and fries that hadn't sold. I rarely eat McDonald's food these days, but I always wished they'd add my invention to the menu. I called it the *Big Filet-O-Mac*. On a Big Mac bun, the bottom half is a cheeseburger, the top half is a Filet-O-Fish. Surf and turf. Very wrong and very tasty.

It was a shitty job from the get-go, but then there was Danielle, redemption in the form of a beautiful seventeen-year-old girl. She was deliberately stunning— the kind of girl you never notice isn't wearing make-up. Our store manager always mistakenly called her Daniella.

They made her a supervisor during my first week and she quickly became my primary reason for staying. The nights I closed the store with her were the best nights of my whole teen life. I wanted to quit high school, move in with her, and schedule naked time together while we ate leftover McNuggets and drank Hi-C from Ronald McDonald's clown shoes. I wanted to learn how to be a man while she became a woman. My only hindrance was her athletically superior boyfriend. *Silly me!*

This guy was probably a douche bag and certainly

a fascinating douche bag. The first of his kind to make me question a woman's attraction to men of this sporty sort. The kind of douche that might be abusive if women weren't so damn independent these days.

He knew I was smarter than him and probably sensed that I was struggling desperately to like him for Danielle's sake, so he usually stayed quiet whenever I was present.

When Douche wasn't waiting around for Danielle to get off work, I was doing my best comedy material for her and the rest of the store as we scrubbed and mopped. Man! She would laugh her ass off. I don't think I'd ever made someone laugh so consistently. So heartily. It was the true sound of beauty and healing, of release and comfort. Danielle was the first girl to show me what I had and how valuable it might be to women.

I don't know what kept Danielle and Douche together, and my only solace was that she always tried to keep a schedule similar to mine because she said she liked working with me. Maybe I was just a little brother, maybe I was non-threatening; either way, we always had good times.

Slow nights were the best. One night, Douche came to get her and somehow, while he waited, we got into a conversation. He told me that Danielle was constantly mentioning how funny I was. I was stunned. She actually spoke of me outside of work, which meant that she thought of me outside of work, which meant that we were at least a little more than just coworkers. That was the moment I knew I'd always love her. That was also the revelation that proved laughter was healing; it didn't have to come from my lungs for it to have a medicinal effect on me. I didn't know how to say these things at seventeen.

I'm sure Danielle is still one of the most beautiful women I could ever hear or open my eyes to, but time changes everything and I have found contentment in the notion that I may never see or hear her again in my lifetime.

In the year and a half I worked there, I got a nickel raise while going through managerial training. There was no moving up. No making ends meet. The owners always bragged about profits while treating their chubby kid to Happy Meals nearly every day. I asked them for a raise and when they wouldn't budge, I finally quit.

I kept Danielle's phone number in my head for some time, but never called. Sometimes memories are so much better than the past ever was. Danielle at seventeen doesn't exist anywhere outside of this text and my heart. It is probably better to keep her there than to ruin it with the of now.

(Some Telemarketing Place); *Telemarketer*
SUMMER 1995
Your basic shady telemarketing experience. On

day two, the boss bought us sushi. I had wasabi for the first time and thought it was mustard. I love mustard. I swallowed a spoonful of wasabi and it set my sinuses on fire. It drained my head of mucus for the next two days. I almost called in sick. I quit instead. I still like mustard, but now I *love* wasabi.

Togo's; *Floater/Broom Manager*
OCTOBER 1995 – FEBRUARY 1996
This is my favorite sandwich place in Silicon Valley. The pay was competitive and weekly. It wasn't your average deli eatery. It was fun. Because of my uncanny ability to sweat from blinking, and because sandwiches were made right in front of the customer, they wouldn't let me prepare food. So all day long I swept, sweated, cleaned, and heated up pastrami. Easy work and I always ate well. The old Vietnamese guy and I were the only ones not on drugs.

Paramount's Great America; *Amusement Park Ticket Taker*
FEBRUARY 1996 – JULY 1996
Within a few weeks, the summer sun gave me a second-degree burn on the back of my neck. I got off work one day feeling heat-exhausted. The back of my neck itched, so I went to scratch it and ended up scraping open a few large blisters. I went home, drank fluids, put on cold cream, and called in sick for the next three days. On that third day, they said if I didn't come in, I was quitting. I didn't come in.

Erik's Deli; *Cashier*
AUGUST 1996 – OCTOBER 1996
My second deli job. My second-favorite deli eatery.
Good employers.

(Some Telemarketing Place); *Telemarketer*
OCTOBER 1996 – DECEMBER 1996
The pay was decent, the company was pretty
legitimate, but I was bored as all hell and most of whom I
called hated me for interrupting dinner.

Apple Vacations; *Operator/Wholesaler*
APRIL 1997 – JULY 1997
The only substantial phone job I ever had. Fantastic
customer service phone training. We sold Hawaiian
vacation packages to travel agents. Travel agents would
call me. I never had to dial the phone. This job afforded me
the opportunity to move out on my own for the first time.
Business slowed so they laid me off. This was the last time
I worked in a cubicle.

Erik's Deli; *Cashier*
JULY 1997 – OCTOBER 1997
My second attempt. In desperate need of employment
and I now lived nearby. Surprisingly got rehired along
with a raise in pay. The owners were awesome. Being
laid off from my last job put me in a funk and I was
unmotivated. I lasted three months, but this led to one of
my longest unemployment streaks, with me moving back
in with my family.

United Artist Theater; *Ticket Boother*
NOVEMBER 1997
I worked for a day…and on my second day I quit to avoid a potential nervous breakdown. It wasn't the job or the people I worked with, it was just me. I couldn't do anything. I was sad and despised myself. My bad for taking the job. The theater closed within six months.

Togo's; *Cashier*
APRIL 1998 – JUNE 1998
This is the second time I worked for this establishment. Different store, same owners. Men of their word. Extremely generous. I worked with my brother and Victor, the general manager. A damn good man and an honest, reliable, sweet soul. He knew how to coax the "sick" into coming to work. One of my favorite bosses, he made labor a little more bearable. I think I still owe Vic twenty bucks. I should give him fifty.

T.I.M.P.A.C.C; *Instructor*
JUNE 1998 – JULY 1998
Theatre In The Mountains Performing Arts Children's Conservatory…I taught kids how to teach themselves voice characterizations and did lessons in improvisation. Good job, got it from a great friend, but I lost that friend due to a squabble over payment. Regrettable. We didn't talk for ten years, but we're good now.

International Magazine Service; *Telemarketer*
DECEMBER 8, 1999
After a long unemployed stretch, I tried my hand at

telemarketing one last time. On my second day, they let me go because they got a "feeling" I didn't like the job. Excellent perception on their part. Turns out the company only lasted a few months after that.

Warner Bros. Studio Store; *Seasonal Graveyard Stocker*
NOVEMBER – DECEMBER 1999
I had always wanted to work the graveyard shift. My buddy Aahz forced me out of being a slacker. Christmas season in a mall is exceptionally weird, but a very interesting study in the human metropolitan existence. I cannot remember if I quit or got fired. They went out of business within a year of my departure.

Kinko's Copies; *Graveyard Copy Consultant*
APRIL 2000 – MAY 2002
Worked with my best friend, Feff, which made it awesome. Learned a lot about computers, the internet, and how to design and print all sorts of things. I had so fun much in that store. Made tons of chapbooks for poor poet friends. Lots of shit to deal with, but definitely the best job I ever had.

First Franklin Financial; *Copier*
MAY 2002 – AUGUST 2002
Got the job due to my Kinko's experience. Got to listen to music while I worked alone. Inhaled black powder toner on accident one afternoon. They fired me for not avoiding accidentally inhaling toner due to someone else messing with my machine.

Century 25 Theaters; *Cashier*
> AUGUST 2002 – SEPTEMBER 2002
> Thought I'd be moving to L.A. so I only stayed a
> month. They showed *My Big Fat Greek Wedding* and a
> Martin Lawrence concert film. BOR-ING.

Kinko's Copies; *Daytime Copy Consultant*
> NOVEMBER 2002 – MARCH 2003
> Same job in the daylight, only much worse than
> graveyard. Day-walkers suck a little more than us night-
> walkers.

Copy Club; *Copy Consultant/Trainer*
> APRIL 2003 – JULY 2003
> Blocks from my house in downtown San José, they
> were trying to compete with Kinko's and they did this by
> charging way more than Kinko's. I realized they wouldn't
> last long, so I usually showed up to work late. I was really
> beginning to despise having jobs. My work ethic was
> shitty and I was not motivated. They finally fired me. A
> week later I won the National Poetry Slam Individual
> Grand Championship. Serendipitous. This was my last job.

Self-Employed; *Traveling Writer, Comic, Poet, Vagabond*
> AUGUST 2003 – PRESENT
> I do not have a job and I hope I never have to get
> one again. I make a living doing all of the things I did
> between jobs. I've seen so much more of the world now.

Best experience I've ever had the privilege to live through. Discovered a lasting work ethic. It's one helluva commute and truly poetic. I was made for this.

AFTERWORD

As a child who had to stay indoors out of fear of injury—feared by me, my family and my doctors—I was left to my room, myself, and my wits. This alone time brought on a fascination with people, stories, storytelling, women, writing, craft-making, music, humor, and performance, which are all of my most current fascinations.

I was surely that kid who made faces in the mirror. I wanted to familiarize myself with everything I could do with my head, just in case I made friends someday and the need for a particular bend of the eyebrow arose, I would be prepared.

Recently, I was reminded of how much I enjoy lip-syncing and to see others do it well. It was nearly impossible to get me away from my record player, usually amplifying Michael Jackson's *Off The Wall*, *Thriller*, or *Bad*, or *Greatest Hits* from Kenny Rogers and Freddy Fender. Mariachi music was also not a foreign sound from bedroom.

I got pretty slick at making it seem as though the puppets I had made were the back-up singers to my rendition of "Man in the Mirror." I rarely ever had an audience so I had to be my own. I entertained myself a lot. I was an absolute dork and it took a long time for me to like that kid, because I guess I could see why no one else liked me. Probably not until high school did I really dig myself enough to focus on other people. When you don't like yourself, you're paranoid, like you have enemies in your hair and in your pockets. You tend not to see others because you're actively trying not to see yourself.

I wonder if there is a connection between daydreaming and not remembering the dreams had when one is unconscious. I usually don't remember my dreams and can say that on average I might remember a dozen a year. However, that number grows as I age. I'll never forget one afternoon when I was around eleven years old, daydreaming in my room, almost a meditation of sorts and I was imagining myself walking all over the walls and ceilings of my house. It lasted for about an hour and whenever I felt low or blue, or whenever I couldn't play outside, I played inside and my house was boundless. I flew to the kitchen to get a glass of water. I jumped onto the roof to play soccer with Johnny Carson. I climbed through the occasional chimney (in the occasional house) and flew to Circus Circus in Reno, Nevada to play video games, hundreds of miles away from home. I even ran the United States of America, as its youngest president, all from my bedroom. I had a puppet vice-president. . . .

I now know none of this is new. Human beings have been doing this since we were fish. But recently I have felt low, and sometimes even blue, and I think so much of it is the fact that I connect with so many people and touch and get touched by so many lives over such little time, that I tend to miss a lot of people when I am home. I miss the people I haven't met yet. I miss opportunities that may never have the slightest possibility of happening. I miss the world I was told about, versus the planet I was given. I have ideas that can change the world, but I need help. No singular entity can do it alone, and certainly, as individuals go, I qualify as singular.

I think as much as possible about the true scope of the world, my place in it, and where everyone I know fits into its cycle. I've been thinking about the friends I once had and those that have adhered themselves to me and my heart. I've considered these three decades of my life and my accomplishments. We let failure, no matter how small, shadow success, no matter how apparent.

Even as a young devout Catholic altar boy, leaning toward priesthood, I knew in my heart of hearts that the only pure reason to exist is to continue existing. To make and make and make—then more so and so on. All that comes before the creation of life and after the creation of life is tangential to the simple cause of procreation. These things that add up to living may aid in this thing called life, but most all of it is unnecessary to the primary goal of begetting. I would rather enjoy begetting, even if it is simply one more of us that I put into the world. Not even necessarily to assume and continue the family name, but to be part of the cycle. To be effective. To push evolution or fulfill the will of the invisible.

I have believed this since just before I was born. It seems simple, but then how could it not be? Were it any harder to procreate, we never would have. There would be thirty-three of us and plenty of parking. War would consist of shouting and handshakes. The birth of a child would truly be a miracle.

McGEE JR: Daddy, why are we here?

PAPA MIKE: To deliver at least one human sperm to one human egg.

McGEE JR: And that's all?

PAPA MIKE: Yep. But you can bookend it with cable TV.

It may not be possible for me to have children due to the damages caused by Spina Bifida. I can try, but it is doubtful I will ever create a life. So imagine my bewilderment—to construct this tiny theory of our place on the planet, then to realize that I can't be part of the grand equation. I'm in no way saying that this theory is correct for anyone else. It is a theory that helps me put together my seven-billion piece puzzle. Also, I have never and will not look down upon or lessen the personal value of those without children, or those who can but choose not to procreate. At this point in my life, if I could impregnate a woman, I would probably choose not to. I would gladly perform everything up to insemination, but I would then yell, "Psyche!" give her a Hug Ten™, then make us a couple of sandwiches.

Suffice it to say, I very much champion those who decide not to be breeders. They're also part of my pinball metaphor. . . .

I came to the conclusion that even though most of us are able to procreate, those that aren't capable are still meant for something. Maybe we're here to guide those who can create into creating. Then once they've done so, we're supposed to let the new person bounce off of us, protect them and teach them how to survive to make more new people.

It is very simplistic, I know, but imagine the world like a pinball machine: Some of us are the knob that's pulled to shoot out the chrome ball. Some of us are the flappers, keeping the ball in play, and the rest are the bumpers, buzzers and lights. We're all working to keep the game from tilting and the ball alive so that we might get more balls.

[Man alive! I wasn't even shooting for the genital pun; that was natural.]

Back to seriousness, my internal clock is ticking, not any faster or any louder than it has before; I think I am simply more aware of it now. I realize that if I am to fit into my own theories and the theories of others that I have implemented into my own life, then I must be the best flapper, bumper, light and buzzer I can be. If people create history, then I'd rather leave my mark on people directly.

This all made feel very sad, overwhelmed and lonely as

I wrote this, but ultimately optimistic for my future and a future I will surely not see.

Whenever I imagine our sun, eventually imploding on itself and putting the lights out on Earth forever, it is a dark feeling that makes me more certain, more confident in my little theory. It makes me sit alone in dark rooms and contemplate the leftover tomorrows we still have to deal with. It makes me long to go back to a time where I don't understand or, at least, long to understand this thing we calling living. I miss being a kid, but I like who I am and how I intend to exist from here on out.

I may always travel and talk to the new and the old. It is probably what I am here for and I am acclimating to this possibility. I am proud to say that I am very good at, for, to, and with people.

I guess being a talking, funny poet is quite the light, flappy, buzzing existence I had daydreamed about so many years ago.

And no matter how much time passes, I do still walk on the walls and fly to the kitchen.

THANK YOU

This is my extended family, recipients of my unending gratitude and love. In order of appearance:

Arthur Flowers, Jack Edwards, Mark Mitchell, Bryan Coy and the Willow Glen/Campbell Coffee Crew. "Feff" Archuleta and the Archuleta family, Bryce Wainwright-Dumont, Melissa Heagerty, Geoff Trenchard, Eric Victorino, and David Perez.

Aahz, Vadim Litvak, icka, William Jeske, Kyle "BB" Bowen, Anthony Miller, Jamie DeWolf, Maranda Collins, Erik Berg, and Ekabhumi. Matt Pignotti, Ben Henderson, RC Weslowski, Rachel "RAC" McKibbens, Tony Brown, Angus "Ms. Spelt" Adair, Cristin O'Keefe Aptowicz, Shappy Seashotz, April Jones, Rives, Rob "Ratpack Slim" Sturma, and the crew of Green Every Monday.

Alvin Lau, Matt Mason, Ed Mabrey, Tazuo Yamaguchi, Joel Chmara, Ken Arkind, Kealoha, Bill MacMillan, Alex Charalambides, Jack McCarthy, and the students and alumni of Plymouth State, NH, Longwood University, VA and CalPoly San Luis Obispo. Frank and Tor Bonham, Dante Maddox, Maureen Hascoët, Elizabeth Murphy, Chelsea Johnson, Jessica Mason-Paull, Johnny Idaho, Elaine Levia and the Levia family, Lucia Misch and the Misch family. Maiya Robbie and her family, Jodie Knowles and the Knowles family, Travis Bilenski, and all of the crew and loiterers at Barefoot Coffee Roasters.

To my fellow douche bag road dogs: Shane L. Koyczan, C.R. Avery, Derrick Brown, Buddy Wakefield, Anis Mojgani, Daniel Leamen, JW Baz, and Robbie Q. Telfer. You are so full of questions, answers, and journeys. I dig that about you and love you with all my heart.

Loads of love to the people from these communities that have housed, fed, and fostered me:

- 🏵 San José, Silicon Valley and the Bay Area (My first love and home.)
- 🏵 Vancouver, British Columbia (My home away from home.)
- 🏵 Worcester, Massachusetts (My new home.)
- 🏵 Chicago, Illinois (My people. My kind.)
- 🏵 Honolulu, Hawaii (My getaway.)

These cities have been havens for me and poets like me: Oklahoma City, Seattle, Bellingham, Toronto, Dawson City, Omaha, Paris, Boise, Ojai, Regina, München, Fayetteville (AR), Rotterdam, Yellowknife, and Southwest England. I implore you to visit, explore, and enjoy. Find the art. Support them and tell them I said "Hello, you sweet nugget."

ACKNOWLEDGEMENTS

All images ©M. McGee unless otherwise noted.

Most of the stories and poems in this collection have been published in these limited-run chapbooks by the author:

333 (2000)
Will Eat For Food (2004)
Pocketful Of Awesome (2004)
Rock the Mike (2004)
Soft-hearted Loudmouths Unite (Limited Illinois Edition, 2006)
No Showers 'til Toronto (with Robbie Q. Telfer, 2008)

An earlier version of "Graveyard Shift" appears in the *2003 NPS Anthology* published by The Wordsmith Press.

An earlier version of "Open Letter to Neil Armstrong" appears in *Spoken Word Redux* published by Sourcebooks.

ABOUT THE AUTHOR

Mike McGee was born with Spina Bifida in Fort Campbell, Kentucky/Tennessee and grew up with a large family around San José, California. He discovered a love of words at age three and now writes and performs everywhere.

In 2003, he won the National Poetry Slam Individual Grand Championship in Chicago, and then in 2006 he won the Individual World Poetry Slam Championship in Charlotte, N.C., becoming the first person to attain both titles.

McGee has served time as a pirate radio station disc jockey, burger flipper, altar boy, travel agent, floor sweeper, hip-hop emcee band leader, voice coach, and screenwriter. Along with Derrick Brown and Eitan Kadosh, he is one of the first American poets to perform at the University of Paris, La Sorbonne. He is co-founder of the living spoken word groups Tons of Fun University (T.O.F.U.) and Solomon Sparrow's Electric Whale Revival.

McGee has a mighty appetite, an uncanny relationship with ladybugs, several tattoos and siblings, and a passable Scottish accent. He breathes somewhere between Silicon Valley, California and Vancouver, B.C. as often as possible, but currently resides in Worcester, Massachusetts. Mike thoroughly enjoys weather, beverages, the number three, and the scent of mock orange blossoms in the spring. Welcome back. Live love. Feel free.

OTHER GREAT WRITE BLOODY BOOKS

THE GOOD THINGS ABOUT AMERICA
An illustrated, un-cynical look at our American Landscape. Various authors.
Edited by Kevin Staniec and Derrick Brown

JUNKYARD GHOST REVIVAL
with Andrea Gibson, Buddy Wakefield, Anis Mojgani, Derrick Brown, Robbie Q,
Sonya Renee and Cristin O'keefe Aptowicz

THE LAST AMERICAN VALENTINE:
ILLUSTRATED POEMS TO SEDUCE AND DESTROY
24 authors, 12 illustrators team up for a collection of non-sappy love poetry
Edited by Derrick Brown

SOLOMON SPARROWS ELECTRIC WHALE REVIVAL
Poetry Compilation by Buddy Wakefield, Anis Mojgani, Derrick Brown, Dan
Leamen & Mike McGee

SCANDALABRA
New poetry compilation by Derrick Brown

I LOVE YOU IS BACK
Poetry compilation (2004-2006) by Derrick Brown

BORN IN THE YEAR OF THE BUTTERFLY KNIFE
Poetry anthology, 1994-2004 by Derrick Brown

DON'T SMELL THE FLOSS
New Short Fiction Pieces by Matty Byloos

THE CONSTANT VELOCITY OF TRAINS
New Poetry by Lea Deschenes

HEAVY LEAD BIRDSONG
New Poems by Ryler Dustin

UNCONTROLLED EXPERIMENTS IN FREEDOM
New Poems by Brian Ellis

LETTING MYSELF GO
Bizarre God Comedy & Wild Prose by Buzzy Enniss

CITY OF INSOMNIA
New Poetry by Victor D. Infante

WHAT IT IS, WHAT IT IS
Graphic Art Prose Concept book by Maust of Cold War Kids and author Paul Maziar

IN SEARCH OF MIDNIGHT: THE MIKE MCGEE HANDBOOK OF AWESOME
New Poems by Mike McGee

ANIMAL BALLISTICS
New Poetry compilation by Sarah Morgan

NO MORE POEMS ABOUT THE MOON
NON-Moon Poems by Michael Roberts

CAST YOUR EYES LIKE RIVERSTONES INTO THE EXQUISITE DARK
New Poems by Danny Sherrard

LIVE FOR A LIVING
New Poetry compilation by Buddy Wakefield

SOME THEY CAN'T CONTAIN
Classic Poetry compilation by Buddy Wakefield

COCK FIGHTERS, BULL RIDERS, AND OTHER SONS OF BITCHES (2009)
An experimental photographic odyssey by M. Wignall

THE WRONG MAN (2009)
Graphic Novel by Brandon Lyon & Derrick Brown

YOU BELONG EVERYWHERE (2009)
A memoir and how to guide for travelling artists by Derrick Brown with Joel Chmara, Buddy Wakefield, Marc Smith, Andrea Gibson, Sonya Renee, Anis Mojgani, Taylor Mali, Mike McGee & more.

STEVE ABEE, GREAT BALLS OF FLOWERS (2009)
New Poems by Steve Abee

WWW.WRITEBLOODY.COM

WRITEBLOODY
QUALITY AMERICAN BOOKS

PULL YOUR BOOKS UP BY THEIR BOOTSTRAPS

Write Bloody Publishing distributes and promotes great books of fiction, poetry and art every year. We are an independent press dedicated to quality literature and book design, with offices in LA and Nashville, TN.

Our employees are authors and artists so we call ourselves a family. Our design team comes from all over America: modern painters, photographers and rock album designers create book covers we're proud to be judged by.

We publish and promote 8-12 tour-savvy authors per year. We are grass-roots, D.I.Y., bootstrap believers. Pull up a good book and join the family. Support independent authors, artists and presses.

Visit us online:
writebloody.com

LaVergne, TN USA
16 August 2009
154905LV00003B/5/P